GRAMMAR: past simple and present perfect

4 **Complete the sentences with the correct form of the verb in brackets.**

1 She ....*arrived*.... ten days ago. (arrive)

2 I .... lunch with Nigel. (just/have)

3 It's the first time I .... in hot springs. (swim)

4 They .... four matches so far this season. (win)

5 It is the third time she .... the film. (see)

6 .... you ever .... parachuting? (try)

7 I .... very upset when I heard she was in hospital. (feel)

8 She .... to Australia three times since the beginning of the year. (go)

9 The last time I .... her was in 1978. (see)

10 I first .... my girlfriend in 1989. (meet)

11 .... she .... her baby yet? (have)

12 The flowers you bought yesterday .... (already/die).

VOCABU ... d

5 **Write th ... with the nouns.**

Noun	Adjective
courage	*courageous*
anxiety	....
bravery	....
risk	....
nerve	....
safety	....
terror	....
fear	....

WRITING: corrections

6 **Underline the mistakes in this student's letter to his English teacher. (There are five grammar mistakes and three spelling mistakes.) Then rewrite the letter correctly in your notebook.**

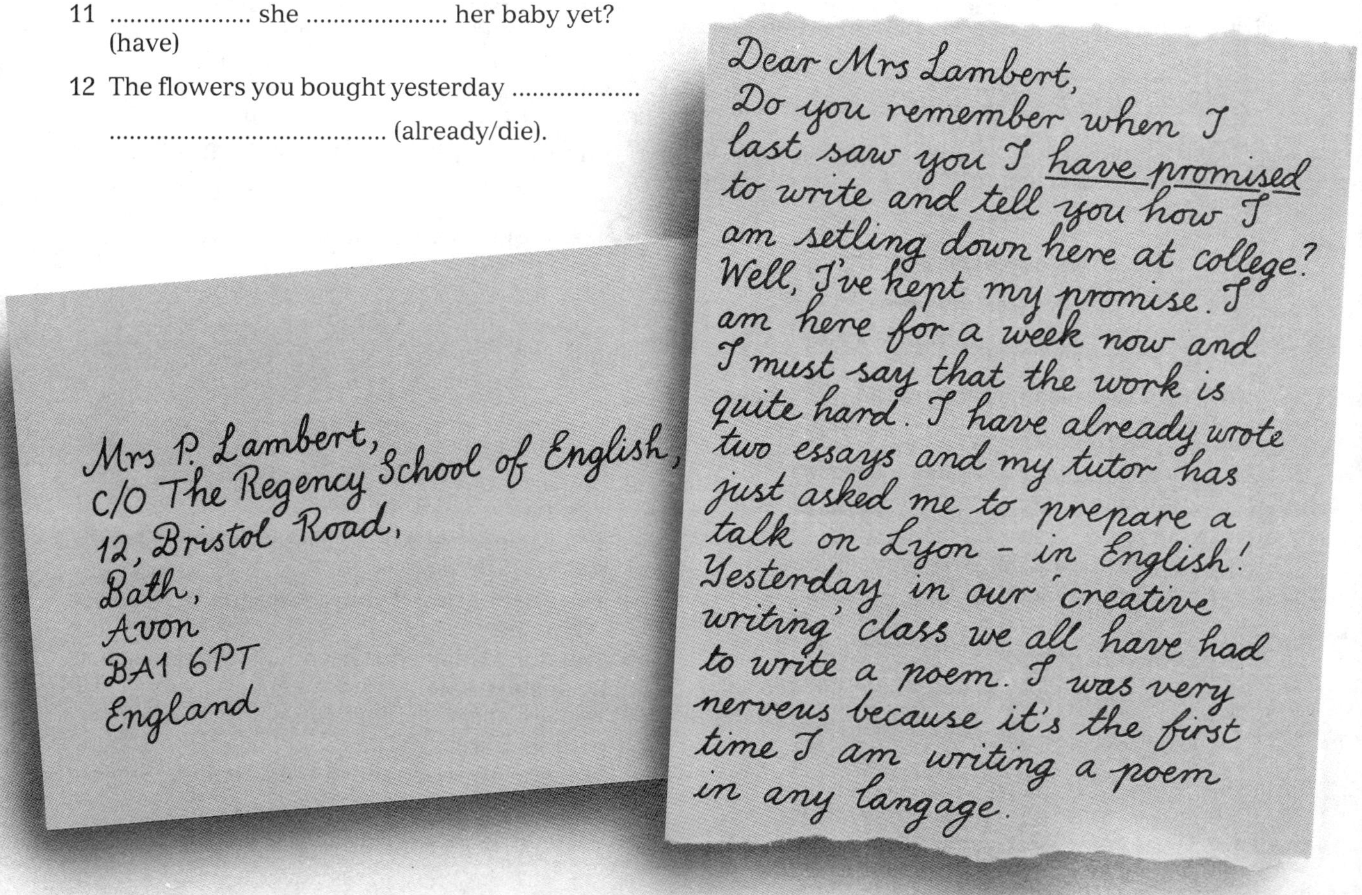

Unit 2

GRAMMAR: question tags

1 Add question tags to these statements.

1 She's not coming, *is she?*

2 They wouldn't like that sort of film, ...

3 She eats meat, ...

4 You won't be late, ...

5 He left early, ...

6 I don't have to jump, ...

7 They haven't replied yet, ...

8 I'm buying the cake for the party, ...

GRAMMAR: negative questions

2 Write negative questions that you could use in the situations.

1 You think you have met the person sitting next to you before.

Haven't we met before?

2 You don't think your friend is enjoying the video you are watching.

....

3 You are surprised that the post hasn't arrived yet.

....

4 You are surprised that the train doesn't have a restaurant car.

....

5 You are surprised that you are not going to have an English test today.

....

6 You comment that the weather is cold for the time of year.

....

ORAL EXERCISES

3 Make comments.

T: lovely day
S: *It's a lovely day, isn't it?*
T: fantastic party
S: *It's a fantastic party, isn't it?*

1 lovely day
2 fantastic party
3 exciting match
4 fascinating documentary
5 incredible story
6 interesting article
7 depressing sight
8 wonderful view

4 Ask questions with certainty.

T: I think I've seen you somewhere before.
S: *Haven't I seen you somewhere before?*

1 I think I've seen you somewhere before.
2 I think we've seen this film before.
3 I think I met you at Tim's house last week.
4 I think that's Jan's new boyfriend.
5 I think she was working in Peru at the time.
6 I think they got married recently.
7 I think you've forgotten something.

5 Ask questions with uncertainty or surprise.

T: You are surprised that John has made a mistake. (John)
S: *John hasn't made a mistake, has he?*

1 You are surprised that John has made a mistake. (John)
2 You are not sure if you and your friend are lost. (We)
3 You're not sure if the glasses are your friend's. (These)
4 You are not sure if your father has phoned yet. (My father)
5 You don't think your friend left the door open by mistake. (He)
6 You are surprised that some friends are getting married. (They)
7 You are surprised that Sue is leaving. (Sue)

Blueprint
UPPER INTERMEDIATE

Workbook

Brian Abbs
Ingrid Freebairn

Longman

Contents

Unit 1

VOCABULARY: dictionary skills

1 **Look at the dictionary entry for *risky*. Then complete the entry for *courageous*. Use a dictionary to help you.**

pronunciation | type of word | definition

risk-y /ˈriski/*adj.* rather dangerous: *You drove too fast round that corner- it was a risky thing to do.*

main stress | example sentence

pronunciation | type of word | definition

cou-ra-geous.kəˈreɪdʒəs..........................

....

main stress | example sentence

READING

2 **In the text below, a young medical student is describing the first time he tried surfing. Complete each gap with ONE suitable word.**

A Narrow Escape

Matthew Hurst describes his first experience on a surfboard

I was 1....on.... holiday in Sri Lanka. I was lying on the beach looking 2.................... the surfers and decided I would 3.................... a go myself. I hired a surfboard and paddled out 4.................... sea. In the distance I could 5.................... the low rumble of a wave. Just 6.................... a moment I saw the beach with its pretty fringe of palm 7...................., then the surfboard stood up on its nose and dived into the waves. I turned over 8.................... over. I had no 9.................... which way was up. My nose was 10.................... of water and my 11.................... were full of sound. The wind had been knocked out of me and my lungs 12.................... bursting. I held my 13.................... for as long 14.................... I possibly could. I held on 15.................... another fifteen seconds. Then another fifteen. I still couldn't get 16.................... the surface. I kept my mouth 17.................... for another three seconds but it was 18.................... good. I couldn't hold on any 19.................... . I gave up and opened my lungs. Then I found myself lying on my side, gasping 20.................... a fish. I had lost the 21.................... but I was alive. I limped back to the beach bar and ordered a soda water and 22.................... omelette. I had 23.................... felt happier to be alive.

GRAMMAR: revision of irregular verb forms

3 **Write the simple past and the past participle form of each of the following verbs.**

	Simple past	Past participle
run	....ran....	....run....
speak	....	....
fly	....	....
drive	....	....
throw	....	....
ride	....	....
spend	....	....
put	....	....
give	....	....
teach	....	....
forget	....	....
know	....	....

Unit 3

GRAMMAR: gerund with verbs expressing likes and dislikes

1 **Write sentences comparing a married couple's different tastes in jobs, routines and leisure activities. Use a suitable expression according to the table below. Look at the code on the right first.**

CODE

✓ quite like, enjoy	× not like, dislike
✓✓ love, adore	×× hate, detest, can't stand
OK not mind	

	SHE	HE
cook	×	✓✓
iron	OK	×
travel by underground	××	OK
watch sport on TV	✓	×
decorate the house	✓✓	××
not have a car	××	OK

1 *She doesn't like/dislikes cooking but he adores/loves it.*

2 ....

3 ....

4 ....

5 ....

6 ....

VOCABULARY: prefix or suffix?

2 **Write the opposite of these adjectives in the correct column.**

Adjective	Add prefix	Change suffix
usual	*unusual*	*—*
thoughtless	*—*	*thoughtful*
careless	....	....
emotional	....	....
harmful	....	....
kind	....	....
original	....	....
safe	....	....
selfish	....	....
tactless	....	....

GRAMMAR: *prefer/would rather*

3 **Write each sentence in another way using *prefer* or *would rather*.**

1 Frank would rather play tennis than play football.

Frank prefers playing tennis to playing football.

2 Jack prefers listening to his walkman to reading a book.

....

....

3 Marilyn would rather go to the theatre than go to the cinema.

....

....

4 Jonathan prefers going out with his girlfriend to going out with a group of friends.

....

....

5 Sam would rather walk than take a bus.

....

....

6 Gillian prefers studying to babysitting.

....

....

LISTENING

4 **Listen to an extract from a radio show called *Find a Friend* in which people use a telephone link-up to find a partner for an ideal evening out. In this programme, Gerry is looking for his ideal date.**

Listen and decide which partner – Number 1, 2 or 3 – you think he decided to choose for his evening out and why.

Number: ....

Reasons:

....

....

....

VOCABULARY: crossword

5 **Complete the crossword.**

ACROSS
1 Two people together (6)
4 Infinitive of past tense *went* (2)
5 She has a horror . . . New York in winter (2)
7 Means *would rather* (7,2)
9 Not together (8)
11 Short for New York (1,1)
12 Likes and dislikes (6)
14 Not well (3)
17 He enjoys staying at home . . . she is fond of going out. (7)

DOWN
1 Usual (6)
2 As 5 across (2)
3 No relationship is ever this. There is always something wrong. (7)
4 They . . . on very well (3)
6 Male subject pronoun (2)
8 First number (3)
10 I'd . . . have fish than meat. (6)
13 Verb form from noun *life* (4)
15 Female subject pronoun (3)
16 He's . . . about tennis. He thinks it's fantastic. (3)

Unit 4

GRAMMAR: the article and zero article (no article)

1 **Complete Andrew's story with the definite article, an indefinite article or a cross if no article is necessary.**

'Saturday, November 15th was [1]*the* sort of day when nothing seemed to go right. I had decided to go to London to buy [2]...... book about mediaeval churches. To start with, I missed [3]...... 9.15 direct train to central London, which meant I had to go a different, longer route via Clapham Junction. Then, when I finally reached London, I found that [4]...... specialist shop for [5]...... books on [6]...... architecture that I had planned to visit was closed. 'Oh well,' I thought, 'as [7]...... winter is approaching, I'll buy myself [8]...... new anorak at one of [9]...... big department stores in Oxford Street.' I bought [10]...... anorak and got [11]...... 3 o'clock train home. After changing trains at Clapham Junction, I was alarmed to find that [12]...... carrier bag with my new anorak was missing. I tried to get another train back to Clapham Junction, only to learn that [13]...... bomb scare had closed every single line to [14]...... station. So I took [15]...... taxi back to Clapham and, as I approached [16]...... station, I saw lots of police standing round [17]...... object on the platform. I recognised it immediately as [18]...... bag I had lost, but my relief turned to [19]...... horror when I realised that it was my bag that had caused [20]...... bomb scare!'

VOCABULARY: word formation: related nouns, adjectives and adverbs

2 **Complete the table.**

Noun	Adjective	Adverb
accident	*accidental*	*accidentally*
....	energetic	....
music	....	....
....	....	emotionally
....	intellectual	....
....	natural	....
....	critical	....
....	fortunate	....
physique	....	....

3 **Use words from the table above to complete the sentences.**

1 She found the literature course *intellectually* stimulating.

2 After her operation she was in a .... condition for several days.

3 Good disco music gives me the .... to dance all night.

4 All new theatres have special access and seating for .... handicapped people.

5 It was a very violent storm, but .... no one was hurt.

6 The country is in the middle of a serious economic ....

7 Unfortunately, Gary didn't have the .... strength to be a dancer.

8 He broke the glass .... while he was washing up.

Unit 5

GRAMMAR: clauses of purpose with *in order to* and *so (that)*

1 Match the two parts of the sentences. Then combine them with *so (that)* or *in order to*, changing words where necessary.

1 The police use hidden cameras
2 She gave me her telephone number
3 Keep your voices down
4 We got up early
5 He shut the door quietly
6 I'm going on a diet
7 Take a map with you
8 My wife's working overtime

a) people won't hear our conversation
b) I want to lose weight
c) we can have a holiday this year
d) I could phone her at work
e) they want to catch speeding motorists
f) we wanted to catch the 8 o'clock train
g) he wouldn't wake the baby
h) you won't get lost

1 *e) The police use hidden cameras in order to catch speeding motorists.*
2 ....
3 ....
4 ....
5 ....
6 ....
7 ....
8 ....

GRAMMAR: present simple and present continuous

2 Circle the correct verb form in the sentences.

1 We generally (*eat*)/*are eating* quite early during the week.
2 Right now I *learn/am learning* to play the saxophone.
3 With regard to my financial situation, for the time being I *work/am working* in a children's hospital.
4 I *am writing/write* in response to your advertisement which I saw in the Daily Times.
5 At the moment I *am enjoying/enjoy* myself in my new job.
6 It is always at this time of year that my family *are visiting/visit* my grandfather's grave.
7 At present I *study/am studying* for my International Baccalaureate.
8 In France people *buy/are buying* fresh bread every day.
9 I *am currently working/currently work* on an alternative energy project.
10 Right now I *am needing/need* to improve my social English for my job.

GRAMMAR: types of phrasal verbs

3 Look at the following phrasal verbs and write them in the correct column according to their type. Look at the examples first.

work out (a problem)	clear up (weather)	
get on with (someone)	look after	
clear up (a room)	wake up	go on
turn off	ring up	

TYPE 1 (T) (⟷) e.g. *get across*
He was good at getting his ideas across.
He was good at getting across his ideas.

TYPE 2 (T) e.g. *get over*
It took him a long time to get over the shock.

TYPE 3 (I) e.g. *get up*
She always gets up early.

Type 1	Type 2	Type 3
work out		

VOCABULARY: phrasal verb: *get*

4 **Complete the letter using the correct form of the phrasal verbs in the box.**

get away	get round	get into	get on
get across	get over		

Dear Uncle George and Auntie Pat,

Well, I have finally [1] <u>got round</u> to writing to you. You'll be pleased to hear that I like it here at Hampton College and I am [2] ________ with everybody, including my tutors! Also, that I have decided to try to [3] ________ university next year.

As you know I had a rather bad argument with Mum and Dad. I just wasn't able to [4] ________ to them that I wanted to [5] ________ from home, and especially life in a small village. Anyway, I hope they've [6] ________ it by now. I write to them regularly and tell them all my news. Anyway, thanks very much for the money. Without it I know I wouldn't have been able to get anywhere to live.

WRITING: corrections

5 **A teacher has circled the mistakes in a student's letter. In your notebooks, indicate the type of mistakes, using the abbreviations below. Then write the sentences correctly.**

Marking Key	
art	= use of article
p	= punctuation
t	= verb tense
sp	= spelling
gr	= grammar
w.o	= word order
exp	= expression
ʌ	= word missing

1 (p) *Dear Sir,*
2 (p) *I would like to apply for a scholarship to study English at your school.*
3 . . .

1-23-8, Uguisudai
Kawanishi-city,
Hyogo, 66-01
Japan

March 5th 1993

The Brighton School of English
103, Fourth Avenue
Brighton
Sussex

Dear (sir,)[1]

I would like to apply for a scholarship( )[2] to study English at your school.

I am a Japanese girl aged eighteen who has just finished (the)[3] secondary school in Japan. Although (I am learning)[4] English for three years, my English is still not good.

(Unfortunatly,)[5] my parents can't (afford pay)[6] (my all)[7] costs and so if I do not get a scholarship I (am not able)[8] to (go England)[9] I like (to studying)[10] English, and at the moment a lot of employers (ask for)[11] English. For that reason, I need to improve my English (for to get)[12] a job.

I look forward to (hearing a good answer)[13] from you.

Yours faithfully,

Hiroe Okada

PROGRESS TEST UNITS 1–5

1 Complete each sentence so that it means the same as the preceding sentence.

1 You're a friend of John's, aren't you?

Aren't you ....

....

2 I'd rather listen to music than watch TV.

I prefer ....

....

3 It's weeks since I had such a good night's sleep.

I ....

....

4 Listening to country and western music is the worst thing I know.

I can't ....

....

5 I've never been to the opera before.

It's ....

....

6 I've never seen such a bad film.

This ....

....

7 She hadn't travelled by plane before.

It was ....

....

8 I'd like to interview him in order to get a better impression of him.

I'd like to interview him so ....

....

2 Complete the sentences with the correct form of the word in capital letters.

1 He won a medal for his .... behaviour. COURAGE

2 You have to be quite .... to parachute from a plane. DARE

3 When I heard about the accident I was

.... very upset. NATURE

4 The doctors say he's still in a .... condition. CRISIS

5 Have you got a satisfactory .... for this? EXPLAIN

6 I must post my .... for a driving licence. APPLY

7 My motorbike insurance has turned out to be

quite .... COST

8 She fell .... in love with him from the moment she saw him. HOPE

3 Circle A, B or C to indicate the word or phrase which best completes each sentence.

1 She was very ... about the row she had with her parents.
A nervous B upset C unfortunate
D frightened

2 She put up a ... fight against cancer.
A firm B bold C daring D brave

3 Could you ... that all the envelopes have stamps on?
A regulate B prove C check
D control

4 When you come tomorrow, can you ... the cassette I lent you.
A take B bring C fetch D borrow

5 What a ... that the post office is shut!
A trouble B problem C difficulty
D nuisance

6 He's received some very ... news about his father.
A urgent B serious C hard D solemn

7 There were three ... in front of me in the queue.
A persons B people C peoples
D person

8 He gave me a beautiful ... vase for my birthday.
A elderly B antique C aged
D ancient

Unit 6

VOCABULARY: parts of the face

1 Write the parts of the face.

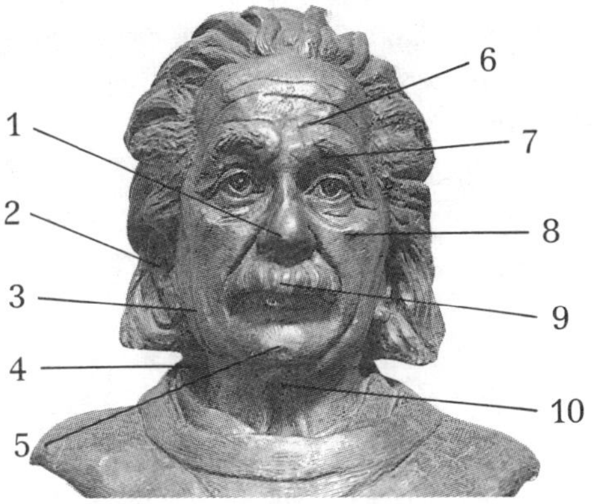

1 nose........ 2 .... 3 ....
4 .... 5 .... 6 ....
7 .... 8 .... 9 ....
10 ....

VOCABULARY: compound adjectives

2 Change each sentence to include a compound adjective.

1 He wore a shirt which had been made by hand.
He wore a hand-made shirt.
2 The sun had tanned her skin.
She had ....
3 The dog had long hair.
It was a ....
4 The man's hair was red.
He was a ....
5 The man dressed well.
The man was ....
6 She bought a blouse which had long sleeves.
She bought a ....
7 He had long hair reaching to his shoulders.
He had ....

GRAMMAR: prepositions with adjectival phrases

3 Complete the paragraph with the correct prepositions.

'I couldn't believe it. Max actually came to the wedding [1]...in... old jeans and a woollen sweater [2]........... leather patches on the elbows! His hair was tied [3]........... a ponytail and he was accompanied [4]........... an older woman [5]........... her late fifties who looked exceedingly glamorous [6]........... a silver bow [7]........... her hair and a red velvet cape. I think more people looked at them than at the bride and groom!'

WRITING: a description of a person

4 Write a description of a person you remember from your childhood. First read the short description below, and then substitute the words underlined with words which describe your person.

Mrs Philips was my music teacher at school. She was *a young woman in her early twenties* with *big, blue* eyes and a *happy* expression. She was *tall and slim*, with *short, blonde* hair. She wore *neat, tailored* clothes and always seemed to be *smiling.*

The following expressions may be useful:

age:	in his/her mid teens thirties etc.	
eyes:	small deep-set	green grey etc.
expression:	puzzled thoughtful etc.	
build:	short	thin well-built etc.
hair:	long shoulder-length	dark red etc.
clothes:	casual shabby etc.	
personality:	frowning worrying etc.	

READING

5 Read the texts A–C and then answer the questions by putting a tick next to the correct name in the table below.

Three famous authors remember their childhood

TEXT A (*taken from 'Boy': Roald Dahl remembers visiting his grandparents in Norway in the 1920s.*)

Bestemama was terrifically ancient. She was a white-haired wrinkly-faced old bird who seemed always to be sitting in her rocking chair, rocking away and smiling. Bestepapa was the quiet one. He was a small dignified scholar with a white goatee beard, and as far as I could gather, he was an astrologer, a meteorologist and a speaker of ancient Greek. The two things I remember most about Bestepapa were that he wore black boots and that he smoked an extraordinary pipe.

TEXT B (*taken from 'Miguel Street': V.S. Naipaul remembers growing up in Trinidad in the 1930s.*)

Eddoes was always well-dressed. His khaki trousers were always creased and his shoes always shone. He wore his shirts with three buttons undone so that you could see his hairy chest. His shirt cuffs were turned up just above the wrist and you could see his gold wrist watch.

TEXT C (*taken from 'The Friends': Rosa Guy remembers growing up in Harlem, New York, in the 1940s.*)

The other man frightened me. He was big. So big that the sleeves of his jacket stopped far above his wrists, leaving part of his large, bony arms and wrists naked-looking like the roots of a fallen tree. His face, too, was unnaturally big. It had harsh lines forming vales along the sides of his nose down to his chin. But then he spoke. His voice, soft and surprisingly high, almost like the voice of a woman, wiped out any idea of cruelty. He smiled and his big dark-brown face crumbled into gentleness.

	Bestepapa	Bestemama	Eddoes	The man from Harlem
Who wore:				
1 black boots?	✓			
2 a tight jacket?				
3 shiny shoes?				
4 neatly pressed trousers?				
Who had:				
5 a heavily wrinkled face?				
6 a deeply lined face?				
7 a scholarly appearance?				
8 a high pitched voice?				
Who was:				
9 wise?				
10 kind?				
11 vain?				

Unit 7

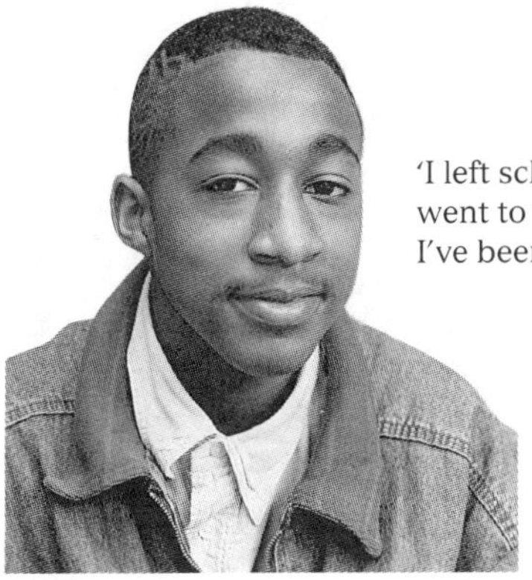

'I left school when I was sixteen and went to work in an electrical shop. I've been working there ever since.'

GRAMMAR: past simple and present perfect continuous

1 **Write sentences about the people in the chart. Write two sentences for each person.**

	Who	What	When	Now
1	Tony	start learning Chinese	two years ago	study it
2	Joe	come to stay	last December	live with us
3	Barry	go to Boston	a year ago	work there
4	Sandra	meet Paul	six months ago	go out with him
5	Peter	get a job at the college	in 1992	teach there
6	Bob	lose his job	they closed down his factory	look for another job

1 Tony *started learning Chinese two years ago and he's been studying it ever since. Tony has been learning Chinese for two years.*

2 Joe ....

3 Barry ....

4 Sandra ....

5 Peter ....

6 Bob ....

LISTENING

2 **Listen to an interview with a man who has just arrived back from New York. Look at the list of stereotypical ideas about New Yorkers, and put a tick next to the ones he agrees with.**

1 New York is dangerous. ☐

2 New Yorkers are rude. ☐

3 They only care about themselves. ☐

4 They talk about money all the time. ☐

5 They're always eating. ☐

GRAMMAR: present perfect simple and continuous

3 **Complete the dialogue with the present perfect simple or continuous form of the verb in brackets.**

CAROL: Do you want a magazine?

TOM: No, thanks I [1] 've read (read) them all.

CAROL: Oh, how long [2] .... (you/wait)?

TOM: I feel as if I [3] .... (wait) for hours but I suppose I [4] .... (only/be) here for fifteen minutes.

CAROL: What time is your appointment?

TOM: I [5] .... (not/make) an appointment. I [6] .... (just/drop in) on the off-chance of seeing someone.

CAROL: Have you got bad toothache then?

TOM: Yes, it [7] .... (give) me trouble for over a week now.

CAROL: [8] .... (you/be) to this dentist before?

TOM: No, it's the first time I [9] .... (ever/be) here.

CAROL: Well, I [10] .... (come) here for about five years. They're very good.

TOM: [11] .... (you/just/come in) for a check-up?

CAROL: No, I [12] .... (lose) a filling so it needs replacing.

WOMAN: Mr Hill, the dentist will see you now. [13] .... (you/fill in) the card yet?

TOM: Yes, I [14] .... (already/give) it to the receptionist.

WOMAN: Thank you. Perhaps you could go up to Surgery 2. Mr Sharp is ready for you.

CAROL: Good luck!

VOCABULARY: phrasal verb: *look*

4 **Answer the questions with the correct form of the phrasal verb *look*.**

What would you do with:

1 someone's complaint about something?
Look into it.

2 a second hand car you might buy?
Look it over.

3 a word that you don't know the meaning of?
....

4 a souvenir that you can't find?
....

5 a painting in an art gallery?
....

6 a mirror on the wall?
....

7 a deep hole or a well?
....

8 a baby if you are babysitting?
....

9 a house or flat to rent?
....

10 a letter after you finish it?
....

Unit 8

GRAMMAR: indirect questions

1 **Change these questions into polite requests beginning with *Do you know*.**

1 What's the time?
Do you know what the time is?

2 When did he leave?
....

3 When does it start?
....

4 How far had he gone?
....

5 Has the bus gone?
....

6 Where was she sitting?
....

7 Did they leave a message?
....

COMMUNICATION: polite requests

2 **Write polite requests beginning with *Do you think you could*.**

1 You want your teacher to check a letter you have written in English.
Do you think you could check this letter?

2 You want a friend to lend you his camera for the weekend.
....
....

3 You want a shop assistant to change a £5 note for you.
....
....

4 You want your landlady to forward your post when you leave.
....
....

5 You want a friend to answer the phone while you are out.
....
....

COMMUNICATION: requests for action and permission

3 **Change these sentences into polite requests beginning with *Would you mind* or *Do you mind if*.**

1 You would like your English teacher to speak a little more slowly.
Would you mind speaking a little more slowly?

2 The music is a bit soft and you would like to turn the volume up.
Do ....
....

3 You would like your landlady to take any messages for you while you are out.
....
....

4 The room is cold and you would like to turn the heating on.
....
....

5 You are in a friend's house and you would like to make yourself a cup of tea.
....
....

6 You would like the telephone company to send you another bill. (You have lost the original one.)
....
....

ORAL EXERCISES

4 Make polite requests. You are making a train journey.

T1: You want to buy a newspaper and you ask another passenger to look after your bag.
S: *Would you mind looking after my bag?*
T2: I'm sorry?
S: *Could you possibly look after my bag?*
T2: Oh yes, of course. No problem.

1 You want to buy a newspaper and you ask another passenger to look after your bag.
2 You ask the assistant at the newspaper kiosk to give you a fifty pence piece in the change.
3 On the train you want to do the crossword in your newspaper. You wonder if your neighbour could lend you a pencil.
4 You feel a little chilly. You would like the person next to the window to close it a little.
5 Your suitcase is on the rack and you would like the person opposite to lift it down.
6 A woman in the corner has got her walkman on very loud. You would like her to turn it down a little.

5 Ask for permission in different situations.

T: You are in a café. You want to borrow the salt and pepper from another table.
S: *Excuse me. Do you mind if I borrow your salt and pepper?*

1 You are in a café. You want to borrow the salt and pepper from another table.
2 You are in a hospital waiting room where there is a TV. You would like to change the channel.
3 You are in the reception area of a hotel. You would like to use the phone.
4 You are on an aeroplane. You would prefer to sit in the aisle seat.
5 You are in a dentist's waiting room. You would like to turn the radio on.

WRITING: a dialogue

6 Write a dialogue for the following situation.

- You are in the departure area at a ferry terminal after your ferry has been delayed. You notice a place next to a woman and you ask if you can sit there.
- You then notice that the woman has a magazine on the seat beside her and you ask politely if she could lend it to you.
- The woman doesn't realise that you are talking to her and you repeat your request.
- You have a portable radio with you which you and your friends would like to play. You feel it polite to ask permission to do this. Tell her you won't play it very loud.

Start like this:

YOU: *Do you mind . . .*
WOMAN: . . .

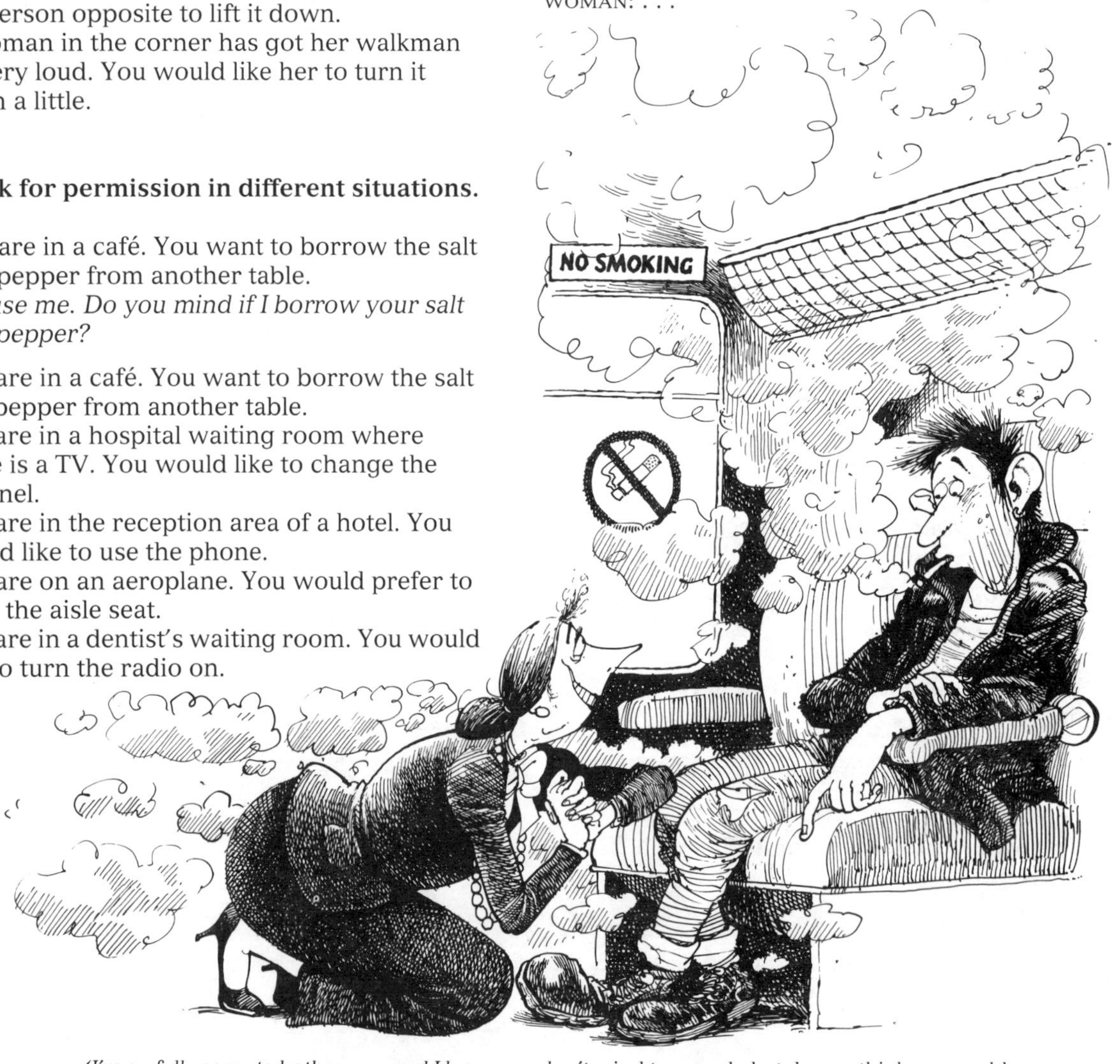

'I'm awfully sorry to bother you, and I hope you don't mind too much, but do you think you could possibly, if it isn't too much trouble, stop smoking?'

Unit 9

VOCABULARY: compound adjectives

1 Write 1, 2 or 3 after each compound adjective, according to whether it describes appearance (1), character (2) or abilities (3).

bad-tempered [2] big-headed [ ] fun-loving [ ]
good-looking [ ] left-handed [ ] open-minded [ ]
quick-thinking [ ] Spanish-speaking [ ]
well-dressed [ ] bald-headed [ ] cold-hearted [ ]
good-humoured [ ] hard-working [ ]
narrow-minded [ ] overweight [ ]
self-confident [ ] warm-hearted [ ]
well-qualified [ ]

2 Use words from Exercise 1 to complete the sentences.

1 In spite of the large number of ...*left-handed*... people, industrial designers still design most tools and equipment for right-handed people.
2 Even though my mother was open-minded about most things, she was very .... about the way her children behaved.
3 Although he dresses casually at home, he's always very .... at work.
4 Despite his reputation as a warm-hearted person, he took some very .... business decisions.
5 Even though he was usually .... at home, he was extremely bad-tempered at work.
6 She was quite a shy person as a teenager but she became very .... after returning from a year abroad.
7 Although he's never been to Spain himself, he has a .... wife.

GRAMMAR: clauses of concession

3 Circle A, B or C to show which word or phrase best completes each sentence.

1 ... being over seventy she is very high-spirited.
A Although B Even though (C) In spite of
2 ... she is well-meaning, she is not always very tactful.
A Although B Despite C In spite of
3 ... his illness, he is self-confident and independent.
A Even though B Despite C Although
4 ... she was the best-qualified candidate, the good-looking man got the job.
A Even though B Despite C In spite of
5 ... he goes to intensive classes, Lineker doesn't know much Japanese yet.
A Despite B In spite of C Although
6 ... having very little money she is warm-hearted and generous to everyone.
A In spite of B Even though C Although

READING

4 Complete the gaps in the letter with ONE suitable word.

Dear Sir,

I am [1]...*writing*... to inquire what has [2].......................... to an order form I completed and sent to your company.

Six weeks [3].........................., on March 21st, I saw a tracksuit [4].......................... your mail order catalogue [5].......................... I decided to buy. I [6].......................... in the appropriate form and sent it with a cheque [7].......................... £39.95, as requested. Four weeks [8].........................., on April 22nd, I had [9].......................... not received my tracksuit, [10].......................... the fact that the catalogue said I would receive it within twenty-eight [11]...........................

[12].......................... leaving a message [13].......................... your answering machine, I have still not [14].......................... from your mail order department.

I am [15].......................... this letter by registered post [16].......................... that it will reach you safely.

I look forward to [17].......................... from you.

[18].......................... faithfully,

John Harris

Unit 10

GRAMMAR: modal verbs of obligation

1 **Circle A, B or C to show which modal verb best completes the sentence.**

You don't [redacted] be qualified to work for us.

A must B got to ⓒ have to

You [redacted] be the right age to apply.

A need B must C ought

If you are keen, ambitious and reliable, you [redacted] to work for us.

A should B ought C must

4 Applicants for this post [redacted] to be sensitive to children with learning difficulties.

A needn't B must C have got

5 You've [redacted] loyalty, enthusiasm and enterprise to work for this successful company.

A got to B got to be C got to have

6 Applicants [redacted] honest, well-organised and responsible people with good references.

A should be B ought to C must have

7 Qualifications are important but you [redacted] have a degree.

A needn't B oughtn't C haven't

GRAMMAR: modal verb: *have to*

2 **Complete the sentences with the verb in brackets and the correct form of the modal verb *have to*.**

1 John is still in bed as he *doesn't have to go* (not/go) to work today.

2 You always .... (show) your passports at the frontier.

3 In your country .... young people still .... (do) national service?

4 Sorry I didn't see you this morning but I .... (meet) my uncle in town.

5 She is one of those lucky people who .... (not/watch) their weight.

6 Soon all art students .... (pay for) their drawing materials.

7 .... you .... (do) a lot of homework when you were in secondary school?

8 I'm so sorry I'm late. I hope you .... (not/wait) very long.

9 Sally's delighted that she .... (not/work) night shifts any more.

VOCABULARY: negative prefixes

3 **Write each adjective with the correct prefix which forms its opposite.**

	un-/in-/dis-/ir-
ambitious	*unambitious*
loyal	
enthusiastic	
experienced	
replaceable	
honest	
responsible	
organised	
reliable	
sensitive	
efficient	

READING

4 **Read the text and complete the chart below with a shaded bar to show acceptable times of arrival for dinner or an evening meal for each nationality.**

	7.00	7.15	Invited time **7.30**	7.45	8.00	8.15	8.30
The British			███				
The French							
The Swedes							
The Dutch							
The Portuguese							
People from your country							

the good manners of arriving

Jennifer Lee looks at the problem of punctuality

Many people often make the mistake of behaving in a foreign country in the same way as they do at home. This can often lead to misunderstandings, and sometimes may even cause offence. Take the deceptively simple question of arriving at social occasions. In Britain, people are quite happy if guests arrive ten to fifteen minutes late. This is the same in France, whereas in Scandinavia it is polite to be punctual. In Holland, however, the time you are invited for is the latest time you can arrive and it is considered correct to arrive ten to fifteen minutes early. A recipe for disaster might be if a Dutch family invited some visitors from Portugal to an evening meal. In Portugal, people do not mind if you arrive half an hour late, sometimes even an hour!

LISTENING

5 **Listen to four people talking about the British police. Tick the person who holds each of the opinions. Some opinions may be held by more than one person.**

Pauline

Brian

Terry

Yvonne

He/she says the police are:

1 not in touch with young people.

2 more visible on the street than the police in his/her country.

3 biased against black people.

4 friendly and helpful.

5 under a lot of stress.

Pauline	Brian	Terry	Yvonne

PROGRESS TEST UNITS 6–10

1 Complete each sentence so that it means the same as the preceding sentence.

1 She's been wearing contact lenses for six months.
Six ....
....

2 In spite of feeling ill she went on the excursion.
Even though ....
....

3 I started going to art classes two years ago.
I've ....
....

4 Could you possibly pick me up at the station?
Would you mind ....
....

5 Where's the information desk?
I wonder ....
....

6 Even though the radio is very old, it still works.
Despite ....
....

7 My advice to you is to see a doctor.
You ....

8 It wasn't necessary to bring a present.
You ....
....

2 Complete the sentences with the correct form of the word in capital letters.

1 The government are unpopular because there are over three million .... EMPLOY

2 I'm not sure she has a .... enough character. STRENGTH

3 If he took more care over his ...., people might take him more seriously. APPEAR

4 I had a very .... night on the ferry. I hardly slept at all. COMFORT

5 Everyone danced .... the whole night long. ENERGY

6 We would like to apologise for any .... we have caused. CONVENIENT

7 I don't know what her .... will be to this letter. RESPOND

8 I'm glad they've decided to be .... about the matter. REASON

3 Circle A, B or C to indicate the word or phrase which best completes each sentence.

1 When we entered the house, there was a faint ... of cigar smoke.
A whiff B scent C flavour D perfume

2 The scientist ... carefully the contents of the test tube.
A glanced at B examined C looked D searched

3 The man was well-built and of ... height.
A middle B typical C mid D medium

4 My cousin has been out of ... for months.
A job B employment C position D work

5 Her new job at the hospital involves ... responsiblity.
A plenty B a lot C considerable D a great deal

6 There isn't enough ... in the flat to have a party.
A place B rooms C room D area

7 It is a ... matter between me and my family.
A particular B private C own D peculiar

8 Do you have any previous ... of this type of computer?
A information B news C advice D knowledge

Unit 11

READING

1 **Read the two true stories and circle A, B or C to indicate the best way to complete the sentences.**

TEXT 1

Letter of the Week

When I worked in Birmingham, I took the same bus to work every morning, met the same people and always sat next to the same girl. We got to know each other better with each journey, and one day she told me she was getting married and invited me to the wedding. Unfortunately, I had to say no because a cousin of mine was getting married on the same day. When I went to my cousin's wedding I was keen to meet his new bride. His choice was excellent. She was my bus acquaintance!

Thomas Julius, Coventry

TEXT 2

Would you believe it?

In 1976 the famous Hungarian conductor Georg Solti gave a performance of Mozart's opera, *Le Nozze di Figaro* in Washington. During the performance Solti accidentally stabbed his forehead with his baton, and blood poured out of the cut. Fortunately, this happened at a time in the opera when only a harpsichord is playing to accompany the singing. Solti ran backstage, got some padding for the cut, ran back, picked up his baton and continued the performance with the full orchestra at the right time. Later, during the interval, a doctor examined him and told him what a narrow escape he had had - his cut was only half a centimetre from a main artery in his head. If it had been any closer, he would have died.

1 Thomas Julius' story could best be described as
A a coincidence B an accident
C a romantic adventure

2 Thomas Julius had been travelling to work with the girl
A occasionally B every week C regularly

3 Georg Solti's story could best be described as
A a coincidence B a disaster
C a lucky escape

4 Georg Solti left the orchestra pit
A while he was conducting the full orchestra
B when only a harpsichord was playing
C after he had finished the performance

GRAMMAR: past simple/continuous and past perfect simple/continuous

2 **Complete the account using the correct form of one of the verbs in the box.**

realise	conduct	run	tell	have
pour	notice	treat	sing	stab

Georg Solti 1 ...*had been conducting*... the opera for some time when he suddenly 2.. that blood 3.. from his head. He 4.. that he 5.............. .... himself with his baton. He 6.. for help while the chorus 7.., accompanied only by a harpsichord. A doctor 8.. his cut and 9.. Solti what a narrow escape he 10.. .

GRAMMAR: past simple and past perfect

3 Choose the correct form of the verb in these sentences.

1 By the time we arrived, they *ate/had eaten* all the strawberries.
2 When I got to the restaurant, I suddenly *didn't feel/hadn't felt* hungry.
3 He was completely out of breath as he *ran/had run* all the way to the station.
4 The children were in high spirits as they *just finished/had just finished* their exams.
5 When the old man *got up/had got up* to speak, everyone applauded.
6 They were chatting as if they *knew/had known* each other all their lives.
7 She wasn't frightened when she saw his cut. She *saw/had seen* blood many times before.
8 When he *saw/had seen* her come through the door, he jumped up in surprise.

GRAMMAR: past perfect continuous

4 Complete each sentence with the past perfect continuous form of the verb in brackets.

1 Simon ..*had been having*.. (have) a bit of a problem with the steering so he took the car in to be repaired.

2 The passengers were fed up as they .... (wait) over an hour for the train to leave.

3 When I looked out of the window I realised that it .... (snow) all night.

4 Real Madrid .... (play) for ten minutes when they scored their first goal.

5 The reason she was exhausted was because she .... (overwork).

6 The moment I entered the room I knew that someone .... (smoke) in there.

7 Ann was in a bad mood at lunch time. She .... (try) to phone the railway station all morning but the line was permanently engaged.

8 Now I know why I couldn't get into the flat. I .... (use) the wrong key.

9 When he got home, he realised that he .... (wear) odd socks all day.

LISTENING

5 Listen to two people talking about an incident that occurred in the middle of the night and number the events below in the correct order.

a) [ ] Roger knocked on Steve's front door.
b) [ ] Roger's dog barked.
c) [1] Roger's wife went to stay with her parents.
d) [ ] Roger went out to see why the dog was barking.
e) [ ] A strong gale started to blow up.
f) [ ] Steve invited him in and gave him a cup of tea.
g) [ ] The front door slammed behind him.
h) [ ] Roger went to bed.

WRITING: a summary

6 In your notebooks, retell Roger's story from his point of view. Use the sentences from Exercise 5 to give you the correct sequence of events. Use the past simple, past continuous and past perfect tense where suitable. Use the following phrases as a guide to help you start.

Let me tell you what happened to me last night. Jenny, my wife, had gone to ...... so I went to bed at about ......
Three hours later ...... so I ......
What I hadn't realised was that ......

Unit 12

GRAMMAR: the gerund or infinitive after verbs of perception

1 **Circle the correct verb form to complete the passage.**

THINGS THAT GO BUMP IN THE NIGHT

It was quite late on a Saturday night and we were having supper in our new house. Things still felt a bit strange so we didn't take much notice when we heard someone [1]*move/moving* about noisily in the house next door – the house was semi-detached. We thought it was a bit strange that our neighbours should be doing their housework so late on a Saturday night but thought no more of it. Then we heard men's voices [2]*talk/talking* softly. From the window I could see figures [3]*move/moving* backwards and forwards in the front garden. We assumed that our neighbours were having some sort of party. Not long after, we heard the front door [4]*slam/slamming* shut. Then complete silence. We thought this was a bit strange, because we naturally expected to hear other people [5]*leave/leaving* and [6]*say/saying* goodbye. However, we went to bed and forgot all about it. At breakfast time, early the next day, we heard someone [7]*shout/shouting* 'Oh no!'. Our neighbours had just arrived back home from holiday to discover that thieves had taken all their furniture and valuables from the house.

VOCABULARY

2 **Complete the crossword.**

1 P	■	2	■	3	■	4			5
U	■		■		■		■	■	
6 S					■		■	■	
H	■		■	■	■		■	■	
■	■		■	7				■	
■	■	■	■		■		■	8	■
9	10				■	■	■		■
■		■	■	11					
12			■		■	■	■		■
■		■	■	■	■	■	■	■	■

ACROSS
- 4 To hit quickly with the flat of your hand. (4)
- 6 Don't . . . . I can hear you perfectly. (5)
- 7 Opposite of *to shut quietly*. (4)
- 9 Many people . . . hands when they meet for the first time. (5)
- 11 To use sudden unexpected violence against somebody. (6)
- 12 Most babies do this frequently. (3)

DOWN
- 1 Opposite of *pull*. (4)
- 2 It's polite to do this before entering somebody's bedroom or study. (5)
- 3 You might do this to a horse to comfort it. (3)
- 4 A good horror film could make you do this. (6)
- 5 A boxer does this to his opponent. (5)
- 7 To take something which belongs to someone else. (5)
- 8 What you do to a football. (4)
- 10 Did you . . . yourself when you fell over? (4)

Unit 13

COMMUNICATION: making arrangements

1 Choose one of the sentences a–f below to complete the dialogue.

a) That's difficult, too, I'm afraid.
b) What about doing something on Saturday night, then?
c) At my place, if that's all right by you.
d) Look, do you fancy coming out for a pizza after work?
e) Sorry, I'm afraid I can't.
f) I wondered if you'd like to come to the health club disco on Wednesday.

PATTY: Clive, (1)...

CLIVE: (2).... I've got to work the late shift on Wednesday.

PATTY: What about next week then? We have one every Wednesday evening.

CLIVE: (3).... I usually do weight training on Wednesday evening if I'm not working.

PATTY: Are you trying to avoid me or something?

CLIVE: It's not that! (4)...

PATTY: Mmm. I really like pizza but I can't. Not this evening. I've got to babysit for my sister.

CLIVE: (5)...

PATTY: Saturday sounds fine.

CLIVE: Where shall we meet?

PATTY: (6)...

CLIVE: O.K. I'll pick you up at eight and I'll think of something fun to do.

1 [f] 2 [ ] 3 [ ] 4 [ ] 5 [ ] 6 [ ]

ORAL EXERCISES

2 Inquire about days and times.

T: You want to know if your friend is free on Wednesday night.
S: *You're not free on Wednesday night by any chance, are you?*

You want to know if your friend is free:
1 on Wednesday night.
2 on Thursday morning.
3 on Thursday evening.
4 on Friday at four.
5 at the weekend.
6 for Sunday lunch.

3 Invite people informally and formally.

T: Ask a friend to join you for a meal this evening.
S: *Do you fancy joining me for a meal this evening?*
T: Invite someone you have met for the first time to come out for a meal.
S: *Would you like to come out for a meal?*

1 Ask a friend to join you for a meal this evening.
2 Invite someone you have met for the first time to come out for a meal.
3 Ask a friend if she wants to see *Robocop 3* with you.
4 Invite some friends of your parents to stay for tea.
5 Invite a business colleague to look round your company.
6 Ask a friend if she wants to go to the jazz concert in the park.
7 Invite your landlady to look at your family photos.
8 Ask a friend to come swimming with you.

4 Agree days and times.

T: Is Friday O.K.?
S: *Yes, Friday suits me fine.*

1 Is Friday O.K.?
2 Shall we say two o'clock?
3 What about Thursday morning?
4 Would three o'clock be all right?
5 How about Saturday afternoon?
6 Shall we fix it for Monday morning, then?

GRAMMAR: *will ('ll)/going to/* present continuous

5 Complete the dialogue using the verbs in brackets and the correct form of *will*, *going to* or the present continuous. The cues in italics will help you.

JOHN: What [1] ...are you doing... (you/do) this weekend, Mike? *(arrangement)*

MIKE: I [2].. (not/do) anything special. What about you? *(arrangement)*

JOHN: Well, I've promised to help a friend of mine, Alison, move a piano into her flat some time tomorrow.

MIKE: I [3].. (give) you a hand if you like. *(offer)*

JOHN: I rather hoped you'd say that!

MIKE: What time [4] .... (you/meet) her? *(arrangement)*

JOHN: I'm not sure yet. I [5].. (give/her/a ring) this afternoon to find out. *(intention)*

MIKE: O.K.

JOHN: I [6].. (let/you/know) as soon as I can. *(promise)*

MIKE: O.K. I [7].. (be) in all evening. *(prediction)*

JOHN: What? On a Friday evening?

MIKE: Yes, I [8].. (watch) the U2 concert on TV. *(intention)*

JOHN: O.K. I [9].. (call) you later. *(decision)*

READING

6 Rearrange the letter extracts below in correct sequence to make a complete letter.

a) My real reason for writing is I'm having a small party here at Ivy Street on Saturday 11th May from 7p.m. onwards.

b) Sunday, April 20th

c) Dear Jan,

d) I'm sorry I haven't written earlier. It was good to see you at the concert last month. I thought it was a great evening, didn't you?

e) Hope to hear from you soon.
Love,
Cathy.

f) Give my regards to everyone at the office and a special hug to Dan.

g) 12, Ivy Street,
Edinburgh
EH3 4PQ

h) The party is to celebrate my new job at the hospital. It won't be very formal so don't wear anything too smart. I really hope you can come. You can stay the night if you like.

1 [g] 2 [ ] 3 [ ] 4 [ ] 5 [ ] 6 [ ] 7 [ ]

WRITING: an informal letter

7 Write an informal letter to a friend similar to the one in Exercise 6. Follow the instructions below.

1 Apologise for not writing earlier and refer to an event you and your friend went to.
2 Give your reason for writing by inviting your friend to an informal event.
3 Explain what the event will be like and who will be there.
4 Express hope that your friend will come to the event. Offer to meet him/her at the station.
5 Send greetings to some mutual friends and anyone else you would like to mention.
6 Close the letter.

Unit 14

GRAMMAR: the article

1 **Complete the advertisements with an indefinite, definite or zero article. Leave a gap if no article is required.**

CALLING ALL STUDENTS

Have you just left [1]...... school? Are you starting [2]...... college next year? Perhaps you are leaving [3]...... home for [4]...... first time? Whatever you are doing, why don't you call in at [5]...... branch of the National Bank and collect your free Student Money Guide? [6]...... guide will tell you all you need to know about organising your personal finances. **Get one today!**

VOCABULARY: expressions with *all*

2 **Circle A, B or C to indicate which words best complete each sentence.**

1 My father doesn't go out much during the week because when he gets home from work he feels ...
A all over B all along (C) all in

2 The announcement of their marriage came ... when we least expected it.
A once and for all B all of a sudden C all in all

3 I think the decision to go to Greece later in the year is a good one. I'm ... it.
A all in favour of B all in C all over

4 Are you quite sure you understand the theory? If not, let's go over it ...
A all in all B once and for all C all along

5 There were one or two problems but I suppose ... it went very well.
A all over B all in all C all along

6 It's ... me whether you come or not. I really don't mind.
A all in favour of B all in C all the same to

WORLD WIDE TRAVEL

WHAT'S [7]...... BEST WAY TO SEE AFRICA ?

Jumbo Safaris can offer you [8]....... holiday experience you will never forget. Enjoy spectacular scenery from [9]...... game reserves of Tanzania and Kenya to [10]...... white peaks of Kilimanjaro. Send for [11]...... brochure now and join us for the holiday of [12]...... lifetime.

DEPT.4, 31 DALE ROAD,
KINGSBURY, WILTSHIRE
SN 13 3QX.

JUMBO SAFARIS

BACK PAIN SUFFERERS

Do you ever suffer from [13] .... back pain? Do you toss and turn when you're trying to get to sleep? Do you dread [14] .... time when you have to go to [15] .... bed?

Have you ever thought that [16] .... problem may be your bed? [17] .... bed that's too hard or too soft can make your pain worse.

For [18]......... good night's sleep, call in and see us at Shopping World in Maldon or phone Comfort Beds 0273 455 5566.

READING

3 **Circle the best adverbial phrase to complete each gap in the story.**

GREAT BRITISH ACTORS

How Sir Laurence Olivier lost his first job

[1] *(At the time)/At the moment* Sir Laurence had a small part in Shakespeare's play, 'Julius Caesar'. They had come to a important part of the play, and another actor was giving an long speech when [2] *at the time/all of a sudden*, Olivier noticed that the actor's underpants were slowly slipping down under his toga. [3] *In fact/In future* they had almost reached his ankles! [4] *At the end/in the end* Olivier had to leave the stage because he couldn't stop laughing. [5] *The next day/In future* the Theatre Manager called Olivier into his office and sacked him for his unprofessional behaviour. [6] *Therefore/However*, it didn't make any difference to Olivier's career. The company wasn't very good and Olivier had been looking a reason to leave [7] *in time/all along*. However, Olivier vowed that [8] *in future/in the end*, he wouldn't laugh at another actor's embarrassment on stage.

Unit 15

LISTENING

1 Listen to Julie recalling some memories of her great-aunt and answer the questions.

1 Is Julie's great-aunt still alive today?

....

2 What contact did Julie use to have with her?

....

....

3 In what two ways would her great-aunt spoil her?

....

....

....

....

4 Why was Julie frightened one night?

....

5 What does she remember her great-aunt doing?

....

....

VOCABULARY: verbs to do with human actions

2 Circle the word which does not match the rest of the group.

1 cheer (circled) pat stroke touch wave
2 dance grab kick run walk
3 hear see slap smell taste
4 howl hum jump sing whisper
5 cough cry laugh sniff shout

GRAMMAR: *remember*

3 Malcolm can't find his wallet anywhere. He is trying to recall how he lost it. Rewrite his thoughts starting each one with *I remember*.

1 I got off the train.

I remember getting off the train.

2 I walked to the bus stop.

....

3 Some boys came up behind me.

....

....

4 They pushed past me.

....

5 I dropped my briefcase.

....

6 One of the boys ran away.

....

GRAMMAR: *would*

4 **Look at the pictures and complete the sentences about people's memories using *would*. Use the verbs given as prompts.**

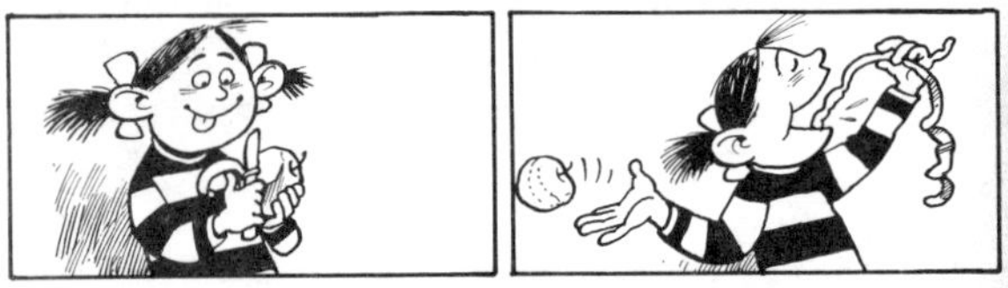

1 peel eat

My sister would peel an apple and then eat all the peel.

2 break drink

My grandmother ....

....

3 talk to

My grandfather ....

....

4 put on

My uncle ....

....

5 read while/feed

My mother ....

....

READING

5 **Read the poem and answer the questions.**

Handbag

My mother's old leather handbag,
crowded with letters she carried
all through the war. The smell
of my mother's handbag: mints
and lipstick and Coty powder.
The look of those letters, softened
and worn at the edges, opened,
read, and refolded so often.
Letters from my father. Odour
of leather and powder, which ever
since then has meant womanliness,
and love, and anguish, and war.

by Ruth Fainlight

Glossary
Coty a brand of cosmetics
anguish pain

1 What did the writer's mother use to carry in her handbag?

....

....

2 Who were they from?

....

....

3 How do we know that her mother used to look at them a lot?

....

....

4 What particular smells remind the writer of her mother?

....

....

5 What do you think happened to the father?

....

....

PROGRESS TEST UNITS 11–15

1 Complete each sentence so that it means the same as the preceding sentence.

1 I ran two miles. Afterwards I felt tired.

After ....

....

2 The moment I saw her I knew she'd been crying.

As soon as ....

....

3 I was watching television downstairs. Meanwhile, a burglar broke in upstairs.

While ....

....

4 Would you like to join me for a meal?

Do you fancy ....

....

5 Would you like me to do the washing-up?

I'll ....

....

6 I dropped my wallet somewhere. I only realised this when I got home.

When I got home, I realised ....

....

7 Whenever I smell newly-baked bread, I think of my mother.

The smell ....

....

8 I used to take the dog for a walk every day when I was little.

I remember ....

....

2 Complete the sentences with the correct form of the word in capital letters.

1 The hotel is full so we'll have to make alternative .... ARRANGE

2 Is March 15th a .... date for everyone? SUIT

3 If he is proved to be ...., he will lose his job. HONEST

4 The amount of luggage she brought is .... BELIEVE

5 It was very .... of you to bring flowers. THINK

6 I don't want to cause any .... complications. NEED

7 I've got to make a short .... at the leaving party. SPEAK

8 Fortunately, I have a very good .... for faces. REMEMBER

3 Circle A, B or C to indicate the word or phrase which best completes each sentence.

1 When we finally ... Paris, we were completely exhausted.
A arrived B reached C got D came

2 I awoke suddenly to ... footsteps in the room above.
A notice B listen to C hear D sound

3 You must ... me to buy some toothpaste.
A remember B forget C remind D warn

4 I can ... something burning.
A smell B sniff C feel D recognise

5 The child spilt the water ... the floor
A all along B all over C over all D all in

6 The thief ... the briefcase and ran.
A gripped B took away C squeezed D grabbed

7 I ... at home all day waiting for them to call.
A remained B rested C stood D stayed

8 You mustn't ... the cat sit on the table.
A allow B forbid C let D permit

Unit 16

GRAMMAR: conditional constructions with *or*

1 Rewrite the sentences using *or*.

1 If you don't give me back the money, I'll call the police.

Give me back the money or I'll call the police.

2 If I don't leave now, I'll never catch my train.

I must ....

3 If they don't come soon, they'll miss the start of the show.

They'd better ....

4 If you don't stop shouting, you'll wake the whole house up.

Stop ....

5 If I don't fill in this form, I won't get a refund.

I must ....

6 If she doesn't turn up on time, she won't create a very good impression.

She'd better ....

GRAMMAR: imperative constructions with *otherwise* and *or*

2 Use the cues to rewrite each sentence linking the ideas with *otherwise* or *or* and a verb with *will* or *might*.

1 Make sure/put the cat out//wake us up in the night

Make sure you put the cat out, otherwise it'll wake us up in the night.

2 Be careful/not/leave your car in a dark side road//someone/steal it

Be careful not to leave your car in a dark side road or someone might steal it.

3 Always/turn the car lights off//your battery/go flat

....

4 Never/drink coffee late at night//not/be able to sleep

....

5 Make sure/get to the winter sales early//all the bargains/be gone

....

6 Make sure/not/arrive late for the performance//not/let you in

....

7 Be careful/not/leave the gate open//cows get out

....

8 Make sure/have an injection//catch cholera

....

VOCABULARY: verbs to do with food preparation and cooking

3 Cross out the word in each group which cannot follow the verb.

1	FRY	onion	potato	~~water~~	fish
2	BAKE	potato	bread	cake	milk
3	GRILL	sausages	egg	bacon	hamburger
4	BOIL	steak	egg	milk	potatoes
5	GRIND	coffee	salt	pepper	cheese
6	GRATE	cabbage	carrot	potato	salt
7	SLICE	flour	onion	bread	courgettes
8	STEAM	rice	fish	biscuits	vegetables
9	ROAST	beef	tomato	lamb	potato
10	CHOP	onion	parsley	nuts	milk

LISTENING

4 Listen to the instructions for making a simple potato and onion supper dish. Number each illustration in the order it occurs in the recipe.

A ☐

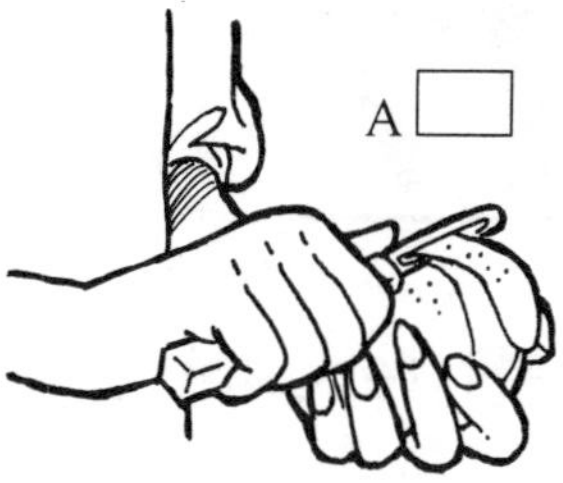

B ☐

C ☐

D ☐

E 1

F ☐

G ☐

H ☐

I ☐

Unit 17

GRAMMAR: reported speech

1 Change the sentences to reported speech. Put the reporting verb in the past.

1 'Go to the end of the queue.' (he/tell/them)
He told them to go to the end of the queue.

2 'I'm leaving in ten minutes' time.' (she/tell/her parents)
....

3 'We don't have enough money to go abroad this year.' (he/say)
....

4 'Who's going to help me?' (she/want to know)
....

5 'Is the station far away?' (he/ask)
....

6 'We met at the sports club last Friday.' (she/remind/him)
....

7 'When will lunch be ready?' (they/want to know)
....

8 'Don't wake me before eight o'clock.' (she/tell/me)
....

9 'You must catch the ten o'clock bus.' (he/say)
....

10 'I've got to phone my parents before I go to bed.' (the girl/say)
....

11 'I haven't been here for weeks.' (he/admit)
....

GRAMMAR: verbs of reporting

2 Complete the sentences with the verbs in the correct form. You may need to add a preposition in some cases.

1 The thief *admitted stealing* (admit/steal) the handbag.

2 She .... (apologise/be) late for the lesson.

3 She .... (agree/lend) her brother the money to buy a sound system.

4 The hotel receptionist .... (warn me/not/leave) any valuables in my room.

5 I .... (suggest/he/go) to see a doctor about his knee.

6 The doctor .... (recommend/take) a long holiday.

7 He .... (promise/take) the children to the beach while I was out.

8 Although I .... (offer/pay) the bill, she .... (insist/pay) it herself.

GRAMMAR: converting reported to direct speech

3 Read the dialogue and then use it to complete Jean's actual conversation with Andy.

Eric and his wife, Jean, are at home when the phone rings.

JEAN: Hello. . . . Yes, he's here. Do you want to speak to him? . . . Oh, O.K. . . . A message? Yes, sure. . . . 7.30 tomorow. And your name is . . . ? . . . O.K., Andy, I'll give him the message. . . . All right, I'll tell him. Bye!

ERIC: Who was it?

JEAN: Someone called Andy.

ERIC: Andy Meyer?
JEAN: I don't know. He said you'd know who he was.
ERIC: Why didn't he want to speak to me?
JEAN: Well, he did but he said he was in a bit of a hurry and so he asked if I could give you a message instead.
ERIC: Oh. So what was the message?
JEAN: He said he'd booked a tennis court for tomorrow at eight and wanted to know if you could pick him up at seven thirty.
ERIC: Well, it's a bit short notice. He said he was going to let me know earlier.
JEAN: Oh, I forgot. He apologised for not phoning yesterday.
ERIC: Oh, O.K. Was there anything else?
JEAN: No, that was it.

Write Jean's conversation with Andy.

JEAN: Hello.
ANDY: 1 *Hello.* ....
JEAN: Yes, he's here. Do you want to speak to him?
ANDY: 2 ....
JEAN: Oh, O.K.
ANDY: 3 ....
JEAN: A message? Yes, sure.
ANDY: 4 ....
....
....
JEAN: 7.30 tomorrow. And your name is . . . ?
ANDY: 5 ....
....
JEAN: O.K., Andy, I'll give him the message.
ANDY: 6 ....
....
JEAN: All right. I'll tell him. Bye!
ANDY: ....

READING

4 Read about a report on women in management and complete the actual words of the speakers.

1 Sylvia Newton, along with a third of the women questioned, has this point to make about working with men:

'We don't ....

....'

2 Damian Rundall, who has a woman boss, makes this negative remark:

....

....'

3 Katriona Philips, a married health service manager, explains why she has had no children:

'..

....'

4 Sally Thorpe, sales manager and mother of two, complains:

'I've had children but..

....'

5 Roger Young, director of the Institute of Management, makes the following points:

'..

....

....

....

....'

The main obstacle to women's progess in business, according to a study published last week by the Institute of Management, is men.

A survey of 1,500 women and 800 men has revealed some interesting facts. A third of the women questioned said they did not receive enough respect from their male superiors, while one in five men said it was difficult to work for a woman manager.

Those women who do overcome the obstacle do so at considerable personal cost. A third of the women were unmarried whereas only 5% of the men were. Many women who were married said that they had decided not to have children because of their careers. Nearly half of the women who were married and had had children said their careers had suffered.

Roger Young, director of the Institute, said that the idea of a 'traditional management career' had to change. He suggested that managers - both men and women - should be allowed to work more flexible hours and to work at home if necessary. He felt that this would enable them to combine work and outside responsibilities.

Unit 18

GRAMMAR: prepositions

1 **Complete the list of tourist activities with a suitable preposition from the box. Use each preposition once.**

round	to	on	through	along	of
in	at				

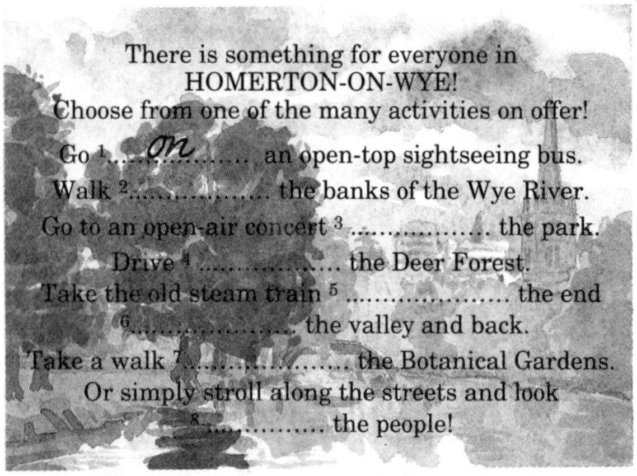

COMMUNICATION: making suggestions

2 **Use the cues below to write conversations. Use the completed conversation as a model.**

1

A: Ask who to get to do some alterations to your trousers.
B: Suggest the drycleaners in Market Street.
A: Say you think they only do drycleaning.
B: Make an alternative suggestion: your sister.
A: Approve of the idea./Disapprove of the idea.

A: *Who do you think I should get to do some alterations to my trousers?*
B: *Why don't you try the drycleaners in Market Street?*
A: *Don't they only do drycleaning?*
B: *Yes, perhaps they do. Well, you could always ask my sister.*
A: *That's not a bad idea. / I'm not sure about that.*

2

A: Ask where to go to buy a good leather jacket.
B: Suggest going to 'Leather World' on the High Street.
A: Say you think it's rather expensive.
B: Make an alternative suggestion: the second-hand market.
A: Approve of the idea.

A: ....
B: ....
A: ....
B: ....
A: ....

3

A: Ask when the best time would be to talk to Mrs Potts (your teacher) about your exam.
B: Suggest talking to her after class.
A: Say you think she is always in a hurry then.
B: Make an alternative suggestion: phone her at home in the evening.
A: Disapprove of the idea.

A: ....
....
B: ....
A: ....
B: ....
A: ....
....

ORAL EXERCISES

3 **Make and repeat suggestions. A friend of yours wants suggestions for entertaining his aunt and uncle for the afternoon. The trouble is, he isn't listening properly when you answer so you have to repeat your suggestions.**

T: What shall I do with my aunt and uncle? (take them for a walk in the park)
S: *Why don't you take them for a walk in the park?*
T: I'm sorry. I wasn't listening.
S: *I said, couldn't you take them for a walk in the park?*

1 take them for a walk in the park
2 go to a concert with them
3 treat them to tea at the Crown Hotel
4 show them the new Dockland building
5 take them to the Botanical Gardens
6 let them have a rest for a change

4 Make suggestions.

T: What am I going to do with myself this evening?
S: *You could always read the paper.*

5 Disagree with suggestions.

T: Let's go to the theatre. (expensive)
S: *Won't that be rather expensive?*

1 Let's go to the theatre. (expensive)
2 Shall we go to the football match? (crowded)
3 What about sitting on the patio? (hot)
4 We could always go on an open-top bus. (cold)
5 Why don't we go up on deck? (windy)
6 Couldn't we go and see the new Finnish film? (depressing)

GRAMMAR: *It's about time*

6 Make comments starting with *It's about time you* . . . using the following prompts.

1 take a holiday
It's about time you took a holiday.
2 give up smoking
....
3 buy a new suit
....
4 see a dentist
....
5 go to the launderette
....
6 go to bed
....

WRITING

7 You are organising a special Saturday evening programme for a group of ten teenagers who are visiting your country. The details are as follows:

You are going to meet the group at six o'clock at their hotel.

You will all have a meal somewhere in town.

The group have to be back in their hotel by midnight.

Write a letter in your notebook to Mr Thompson, the leader of the group, to confirm the arrangements for the evening.

PARAGRAPH 1
Say how much you are looking forward to meeting the group (say when) and say why you are writing.

PARAGRAPH 2
Say what time you will meet the group at their hotel and what you are going to do in the evening.

PARAGRAPH 3
Say you hope the day will be a great success and promise to make sure the group are back at the hotel at the arranged time.

Start like this:
Dear Mr Thompson,
I'm looking forward to . . .

Unit 19

VOCABULARY: types of film

1 **Which types of film do you associate with the following actors, directors or titles? Sometimes more than one answer is possible.**

horror film   western   adventure film comedy   science fiction film   police drama animated film   psychological thriller

1 Clint Eastwood ..*western,*..........................
....
2 Walt Disney ....
3 *Dracula* ....
4 Steven Spielberg ....
5 *Star Wars* ....
6 Alfred Hitchcock ....
7 *Robocop* ....
....
8 Woody Allen ....

VOCABULARY: nouns and adjectives

2 **Complete the list with the missing noun or adjective.**

Noun	Adjective
sentiment	..*sentimental*..
history	....
....	romantic
....	psychological
....	humorous
confusion	....
animation	....
....	surprising
criticism	....
fiction	....

READING

3 **Read the story and circle A, B or C to indicate the best answer.**

The case of the disappearing garden

A year ago, Mr and Mrs Ratcliffe decided to leave London and bought a house in a village in Cornwall. Everything was wonderful to begin with but then things started to happen. Soon deep puddles began to appear in the garden even when there hadn't been any rain. They thought that maybe the earth was very soft and that it was sinking naturally. Then, after a few weeks, they noticed cracks appearing in the walls inside the house. At first they weren't particularly worried because it was a new house and people say that new plaster always cracks when 'settling down'. Then, one morning, Mrs Ratcliffe heard a strange rumbling noise and woke up to find that part of the garden had disappeared! She quickly woke her husband, grabbed the children and ran. No sooner had they reached the front gate than the whole garden disappeared completely into an enormous hole.

Not long after, the council admitted that the house had been built over an old, disused tin mine which had been closed over a hundred years ago. The house is being surveyed at the moment, and Mr and Mrs Ratcliffe are still waiting to hear whether or not it's safe for them to move back in.

1 Mr and Mrs Ratcliffe became alarmed when they saw deep puddles appearing in the garden
A after it had rained.
B after only a very small amount of rain.
C although it hadn't rained at all.

2 When they saw cracks in the walls of the house
A they were immediately concerned.
B they didn't worry too much.
C they decided to get some new plaster to cover the cracks.

3 They realised they were in danger when
A the plaster cracked completely.
B their house collapsed.
C some of their garden fell into a hole.

4 The council
A were aware of the mine being under the house.
B never knew anything about the mine under the house.
C said that the couple should have chosen a different house in another part of the village.

Unit 20

GRAMMAR: revision of reported speech

1 Rewrite these sentences from an extract from *Jane Eyre* as reported speech.

1 'Give me the water, Mary,' he said. (tell)
He told Mary to give him the water
2 'What is the matter?' Rochester inquired. (ask)
....
3 'I will carry it in,' she said. (say)
....
4 'Answer me – speak again!' he ordered. (order/Jane)
....
....
5 'I cannot see you but I must touch you' he said to Jane. (say)
....
....
6 'I spilt half of what was in the glass,' I said. (she/say)
....
....

LISTENING: animals and their sounds

2 Listen and name the animal and the sound it is making.

1 It's a cow. It's mooing.
2 ....
3 ....
4 ....
5 ....
6 ....
7 ....
8 ....

VOCABULARY: verbs and parts of the body

3 Use the pictures to complete each sentence.

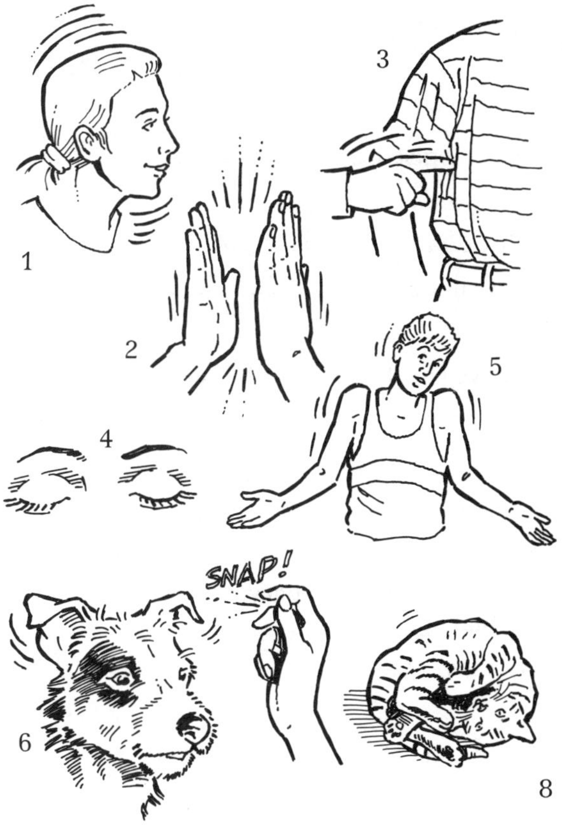

1 She nodded her head in agreement when he made the point.
2 They .... with excitement when they saw their presents.
3 It's annoying the way he always .... people ....
4 I told her to .... and I would give her a surprise present.
5 When I asked him the reason, he simply
....
6 The dog always .... ears when it hears someone at the door.
7 He .... at the waiter.
8 The cat loves to .... by the fire on a cold evening.

PROGRESS TEST UNITS 16–20

1 Complete each sentence so that it means the same as the preceding sentence.

1 'I can't come tomorrow,' she said.

She said that ....

....

2 'I'm sorry I was rude,' he said.

He apologised ....

....

3 'Why don't we go to the police?'

They suggested ....

....

4 'You've cheated, John!' she said.

She accused ....

....

5 I recommend seeing the new musical.

You ....

6 If you don't give me back my money, I'll call the manager.

Give me ....

....

7 Never put cash in your back pocket.

Make sure ....

....

8 Pour some oil in the pan, otherwise the mixture will stick.

If you ....

....

2 Complete the sentences with the correct form of the word in capital letters.

1 Unfortunately, students are often .... about their spelling in exams. CARE

2 I chose the restaurant on the .... of friends. RECOMMEND

3 Sometimes the film was so .... I couldn't look at the screen. FRIGHT

4 We saw a wonderful .... of the ballet, *Swan Lake*. PERFORM

5 She was one of the most .... members of the group. LIVE

6 Nowadays young people like films with plenty of .... ACT

7 The committee are going to make their .... tomorrow. DECIDE

8 His .... to listen to advice is his main problem. REFUSE

3 Circle A, B, or C to indicate the word or phrase which best completes each sentence.

1 I'm going ... a cake for tea.
A cook B roast C heat D bake

2 The dog ... angrily and loudly when it saw the postman.
A barked B yelped C roared
D howled

3 When I asked him who he'd been talking to, he just ... his shoulders.
A lifted B raised C shrugged
D shook

4 In our English course, we're going to study the English ... .
A story B novel C book D literature

5 Someone is coming from the police tomorrow to ... to us about crime prevention.
A talk B say C tell D announce

6 If you're ill, I ... you see a doctor.
A advise B suggest C warn D tell

7 I was a bit nervous ... but I soon started to enjoy myself.
A firstly B at first C first
D in the beginning

8 I waited half an hour for a bus but ... I took a taxi.
A in the end B at the end C finally
D consequently

Unit 21

VOCABULARY: phrasal verbs: money and spending

1 Read and complete the text using the correct form of one of the phrasal verbs from the box.

run out of	pay into	pay for	live on
save up	pay back		

Jim is a student at Manchester University. At the beginning of term he gets a grant cheque which he 1 ..*pays into*.. his bank account. This is supposed to be enough to 2 .... for about three months. However, by the time he has paid his rent and his bills and 3 .... all the money he owes to his friends, he has very little left. By the middle of term he has usually 4 .... money! He is hoping to go on holiday to Nepal in the summer but he is not sure if he will be able to 5 .... enough money to 6 .... it.

VOCABULARY: abstract nouns

2 Complete the sentences by making an abstract noun from the adjectives in brackets.

1 Mike is well-known for his .*generosity*..... when it comes to giving presents. (GENEROUS)

2 Bob has always felt a strong sense of .... towards the people he employs. (LOYAL)

3 The architect's plans showed a definite lack of .... (IMAGINATIVE)

4 My aunt has an .... about .... and cleans the whole house from top to bottom every day. (OBSESSIVE/TIDY)

5 Sam's latest .... is a pair of very expensive trainers. (EXTRAVAGANT)

6 Their new car made them the .... of the whole neighbourhood. (ENVIOUS)

7 One reason for his .... is that his own father was very stingy. (MEAN)

8 Being a good secretary requires a lot more .... than most people realise. (INTELLIGENT)

GRAMMAR: prepositions after abstract nouns

3 Circle the correct preposition in these sentences.

1 There has been a substantial fall *of*/(in) temperature this week.
2 Did you hear the result *of/from* the football match?
3 They have made an urgent request *to/for* international aid.
4 There has been no improvement *in/of* his health since Monday.
5 What sort of relationship do you have *to/with* your parents?
6 The solution *to/of* the problem is quite simple: we need more time.
7 Have you had any more complaints *with/about* the food?
8 I am shocked at the increase *in/of* the price of CDs.

Unit 22

GRAMMAR: first and second conditional clauses

1 **Complete the sentences with the correct form of the verb in brackets.**

1 If you can lend me £10, I ...'ll pay... (pay) you back tomorrow.

2 John would probably have to borrow money from the bank if his parents ...didn't... ...give... (not/give) him extra money every month.

3 Don't worry. My parents ...didn't mind... (not/mind) if you stay the night.

4 ...would... (you/buy) the shoes if they were in the sale?

5 I ...will definitely... (definitely/have) a party if I pass all my exams.

6 I'd come with you to the film if it ...didn't... ...finish... (not/finish) so late.

7 If I didn't have extra English lessons, I ...wouldn't be... (not/be able to) stay in this class.

8 How ...will you get... (you/get) home if you missed the last train?

GRAMMAR: conditionals with *unless/as long as/ provided (that)/ even if*

2 **An English language school have asked students their opinions about some proposed improvements. Here are some answers. Choose the correct conditional expression to complete them.**

COMPUTERS
1

Yes, I would use the computers after school, (as long as/even if) there were a teacher there to help me.

EXCURSIONS
2

No, I would not want to take part in school excursions, (provided that/unless) they took place at the week-end.

VIDEO
3

Yes, I would like to have a video lesson once a week (unless/provided that) it were related to the course-work.

CANTEEN PRICES
4

I always bring a packed lunch, so I would not eat in the canteen (even if/ as long as) it were much cheaper.

END-OF-TERM PARTY
5

Yes, I would come along to a party at the end of term (provided that/unless) I could bring a friend.

TESTS
6

Yes, I would find it helpful to have regular tests (unless/as long as) the teacher gave us time to prepare for them.

3 **Sue is a young mother talking to Mrs Davis, a careers adviser, about the possibility of training as a nurse. Complete the dialogue using the correct form of the verb in brackets.**

SUE: I'm thinking of training as a nurse. What do you think?

MRS D: It depends. Would you mind working long hours?

SUE: No, I [1]...*wouldn't mind*... (not/mind) as long as I [2]........................ (enjoy) the work.

MRS D: Could you work at weekends?

SUE: Yes, I [3]........................ (can), provided that I [4]........................ (have) some time off during the week.

MRS D: How would you feel about working overtime?

SUE: That would be O.K. as long as I [5]................. (be) paid for it.

MRS D: Could you work at nights?

SUE: Probably not, unless I [6] ....

.... (be able to) get someone to baby-sit.

MRS D: Wouldn't your husband look after the children?

SUE: I suppose he might, provided I [7].................. (pay) him!

LISTENING

4 Listen to a conversation in a shop and answer the questions.

1 What is the girl buying?

....

2 How much does the item that the sales assistant shows her cost?

....

3 Under what three conditions can she return the item?

a) Provided that she ....

....

....

b) ....

....

....

c) ....

....

....

READING

5 Read the text and circle a), b) or c) to indicate the correct answer.

1 To get four free CDs all you have to do is
a) fill in a membership form.
b) buy one CD and agree to buy five more.
c) buy one CD for £12.99.

2 If you want to cancel your membership after a year, all you do is
a) telephone the club.
b) write to the club.
c) send the club a notice.

3 Imagine you have become a member and you have just received your introductory offer of four CDs. You are not satisfied with the goods and want to cancel your membership. When is the earliest you can do this?
a) in one month's time
b) in six months' time
c) immediately, as long as you return all your CDs within ten days.

Unit 23

ORAL EXERCISES

1 Express approval and disapproval (1)

T: What did you think of the film?
(X see this year)
S: *I didn't think much of it, actually. In fact, it's one of the worst films I've seen this year.*
T: What did you think of the restaurant?
(✓ ever go to)
S: *I was quite impressed by it, actually. In fact, it's one of the best restaurants I've ever been to.*

1 What did you think of the film?
(X see this year)
2 What did you think of the restaurant?
(✓ ever go to)
3 What did you think of the book? (✓ ever read)
4 What did you think of the documentary?
(X see this year)
5 What did you think of the hotel? (✓ ever stay in)
6 What did you think of the concert?
(✓ go to this year)
7 What did you think of the meal? (X ever have)

2 Express approval and disapproval (2)

T: Did you enjoy the meal?
(first course excellent/main course not very interesting)
S: *I thought the first course was excellent but I didn't think the main course was very interesting.*

1 Did you enjoy the meal?
(first course excellent/main course not very interesting)
2 Did you enjoy the film? (story O.K./acting not very impressive)
3 Did you like the hotel? (rooms comfortable/ service not very efficient)
4 What did you think of the concert? (first half excellent/second half not very exciting)
5 How did you like the car? (design very elegant/ performance not very impressive)

GRAMMAR: past modal simple

3 Write the past modal simple form of the verbs below.

1 should see .... *should have seen*
2 should ring ....
3 ought to catch ....
4 shouldn't oversleep ....
....
5 oughtn't to make ....
....
6 should buy ....
7 ought to tell ....

GRAMMAR: past modal continuous

4 Look at the pictures and say what the people were doing wrong in each case. Write sentences using the prompts below the pictures.

1 (speak Spanish)
They shouldn't have been speaking Spanish.

2 (study for his exams)
He ....
....

3 (wear ties)

They ....

....

4 (climb in those conditions)

They ....

....

5 (cycle on the pavement)

He ....

....

6 (smoke)

They ....

....

GRAMMAR: expressing cause and effect

5 **Mrs Ives is a pensioner who plays the violin. After attending a Music Summer School in York, Mrs Ives wrote to Mr Shaw, the course director, to express her appreciation. Complete the letter by filling in the gaps with an appropriate adverbial linking phrase from the box.**

nevertheless	but on the whole	in fact
as a result	because of	

Dear Mr Shaw,

I am writing to congratulate you on the very successful Summer School you organised in York this year.

I must confess, at first I was a bit apprehensive about taking part in a course like yours 1 because of my age (I am now 65 years old)! The majority of students were, indeed, much younger than me, but, 2 ...., I always felt very much part of the group. 3 ...., everybody was very friendly and encouraging, especially the staff. The teaching was of an exceedingly high standard and, 4 ...., my technique and general performance have improved enormously.

My only complaint is that such a full time-table left very little free time, 5 .... I spent a very enjoyable two weeks and I hope to come back again next year.

Yours sincerely,

Margaret Ives (Mrs)

WRITING: a letter of appreciation

6 **Write a similar letter of appreciation in your notebooks. Use the notes below.**

- just been on an painting course
- worried about your inexperience
- quite a few of the people on the course already established artists
- didn't turn out to be a problem
- many of the others nervous too
- teaching very impressive
- learnt a lot of new techniques
- only complaint: inconvenient meal times

Unit 24

GRAMMAR: *if only/I wish* + past simple/past perfect

1 **Look at the pictures and write sentences using *I wish* or *If only* according to the cues below the pictures.**

1 wish/not/eat all that ice cream

I wish I hadn't eaten all that ice-cream.

2 If only/have enough money to redecorate the house

3 wish/not/have to spend so long commuting to work every day

4 If only/not/forget to lock the door

5 wish/can/remember the number of the house

6 wish/she/tell me she hated classical music

7 If only/not/drop out of college

GRAMMAR: the third conditional

2 Write what you would say in these situations, using the third conditional.

1 You have made some soup for supper. Your brother comes back with three friends. He didn't tell you he was going to do this and you don't have enough soup for everyone. What do you say to your brother?

If you'd told me you were going to invite three friends to supper, I'd have made some more soup.

2 You were in the shower when the telephone rang so you didn't answer it. Your mother told you later that it was her on the phone and wondered why you hadn't answered it. What do you say to her?

....

....

....

3 A friend has just reminded you that there is a party on Saturday night. You nearly forgot about it. What do you say to your friend?

....

....

....

4 A friend is upset because when you visited his home town last week you didn't visit him. Unfortunately, you didn't have time. What do you say to him?

....

....

....

5 Your younger sister took a photo of her best friend but unfortunately she stood too close so the photo wasn't very good. What do you say to her?

....

....

....

6 A company offered you a job but the salary was very low. You didn't take the job. Your father wonders why. What do you say to him?

....

....

....

VOCABULARY: verb or noun?

3 Complete the sentences using a word from the list below in either its noun or verb form.

heat	fire	trace	claim	crash
burn	spark			

1 For lunch he ...*heated*... up the pizza that was left over from yesterday.

2 When her video was stolen, Kate was able to .... the money back on her insurance.

3 In spite of a great deal of publicity, the police were unable to .... the stolen goods.

4 She sat under the beach umbrella as she couldn't stand the ....

5 The mention of nuclear weapons was enough to .... off a very animated discussion.

6 The heat from the .... was so intense that nobody could go near it.

7 The hospital treated him for the .... on his arm.

8 She accidentally dropped the mug and it fell to the ground with a loud ....

9 The bank robber .... his gun twice to warn everyone not to move.

10 There's nothing to eat. I'm afraid I .... the dinner!

LISTENING

4 Listen to the travel story and complete the sentences using a third conditional.

1 If he *hadn't had* plenty of time, he would have missed the plane altogether.

2 He would never have contacted his wife if his colleague .... him to wait.

3 If his wife .... the house, she would have answered the phone earlier.

4 If his wife hadn't left the window open, she .... the phone ringing.

5 His wife .... to the airport in time if they had lived further from the airport.

Unit 25

READING

1 Read the story and answer the questions.

KIDNAP!

Mr and Mrs Barker were having a quiet day at home. Their 17-year-old daughter was away in Scotland staying with a friend. At 12 noon, Mr and Mrs Barker *got* a phone call from the friend where their daughter was supposed to be staying, saying that she had disappeared. They were just about to call the police when the phone rang again. A hoarse voice *told* Mr Barker that his daughter had been kidnapped and that unless he paid a ransom of £1,000, he would never see his daughter alive again. When Mr Barker *asked* who the caller was, the voice *answered* that it was someone he knew well. The voice then gave him instructions about where and when to hand over the money. He was warned not to tell the police or to *try* to have the phone call traced.

Mr Barker went to the bank and immediately *took* the money *out* of his bank account and left on the next train to Brighton. When he arrived, he *went into* the Grand Hotel at five to six and carefully *put* the briefcase beside a sofa as arranged. At 6 o'clock precisely, a woman in a scarf and raincoat *came up*, took the briefcase and walked quickly away.

At 10 p.m. the same evening, to his great relief, his daughter *came back* home. She could hardly *stop herself from* laughing. Imagine his surprise when she handed him his briefcase containing the £1,000. It *turned out* that she and her friend had decided to play a practical joke. It was she who had put on a hoarse voice to phone her father and it was she who had collected the briefcase in Brighton. The joke had *worked* but, strangely enough, Mr and Mrs Barker did not *enjoy* it as much as their daughter did!

1 Where was Mr and Mrs Barker's daughter supposed to be?
In Scotland. ....

2 What did the daughter's friend phone to say?
....

3 What did the second person phone to say?
....

4 How much did the person want in ransom money?
....

5 Where did Mr Barker have to go with the money?
....

6 Where did he put the money?
....

7 At what time was the briefcase collected?
....

8 What happened at 10 p.m. the same evening?
....

9 What did she give her father?
....

10 What was her explanation?
....
....
....

VOCABULARY: formal and informal register

2 Rewrite the story in your notebook, replacing the verbs underlined by a more formal equivalent from the list below.

return	enter	approach	inquire
inform	receive	attempt	appreciate
reply	refrain from	place	transpire
withdraw	succeed		

GRAMMAR: *look/look as if/look like*

3 Look at the picture and the cues. Make sentences with *look, look like* or *look as if*.

1 She looks like .... my Aunt Agatha.
2 .... she's going to have tea with the Queen.
3 .... awful.
4 .... she's swallowed something nasty.
5 .... very uncomfortable.
6 .... an actress.

PROGRESS TEST UNITS 21–25

1 Complete each sentence so that it means the same as the preceding sentence.

1 The number of people over the age of eighty has increased considerably.

There has ....

....

2 Some people are complaining about the canteen food.

There have ....

....

3 I won't come if I don't get paid.

Unless ....

....

4 The breakfasts weren't very good.

I didn't think much ....

5 He was stupid to leave without a map.

He shouldn't ....

....

6 Because he had broken his leg, he couldn't come trekking with us.

Because of ....

....

7 Had there not been a lifeguard on the beach, she might have drowned.

If ....

....

8 It was stupid of me not to listen to my mother's advice.

I wish ....

....

2 Complete the sentences with the correct form of the word in capital letters.

1 The school won't put up with her bad

.... any longer. BEHAVE

2 He made a .... recovery after his operation. REMARK

3 Unfortunately, his attempt to break the world

record was .... SUCCEED

4 The police have set up an .... into the bank fraud. INQUIRE

5 She didn't pass her exam because her revision

was so .... ORGANISE

6 She developed an .... about a young Hollywood actor. OBSESSIVE

7 We used to drop in and see her

.... on our way home from school. OCCASION

8 The children went to bed early but they were

too .... to sleep. EXCITE

3 Circle A, B or C to indicate the word or phrase which best completes each sentence.

1 You won't ... very much money in that kind of job.
A win b gain C earn D receive

2 The company is not going to make much ... in the first year.
A fee B reward C profit D expense

3 We'd like you to pay the ... sum in advance.
A whole B all C half D finished

4 The government are trying to encourage people to ... money.
A waste B spare C save D keep

5 The problem was that they got into ... soon after they married.
A debt B fine C fee D tax

6 She has a house in Los Angeles and leads a very ... lifestyle.
A generous B extravagant C mean
D well-off

7 Could you speak up please? We can ... hear you.
A almost B nearly C hardly D never

8 It was nothing special, just a ... day.
A usual B plain C common D normal

Unit 26

GRAMMAR: future perfect

1 Make responses to the statements or questions, using the cues and the future perfect.

1 A: Is it all right if I get to the cinema at 7.30?
B: No, I'm afraid that's too late. The film/start/ by then.
No, I'm afraid that's too late. The film will have started by then.

2 A: I hear Sue and John are moving to Paris next month.
B: Sue/have the baby/by then?
....
....

3 A: I'll be at your house at eight o'clock. O.K?
B: Actually, could you make it a little later? I don't expect we/finish eating/by then.
....
....
....

4 A: Only one more week's holiday!
B: It's just as well. We/run out of money/by next week.
....
....

5 A: I'd better sign that letter before I go off to lunch.
B: I'm afraid I/not/type it/by lunchtime.
....
....

6 A: It'll be nice to see Malcolm again. Shall I come round in half an hour?
B: He/not/arrive/by then, I'm afraid.
....
....

7 A: I've got to give that book back to the library next Monday.
B: That's rather soon. You/read it/by Monday?
....
....

VOCABULARY: prefixes

2 Match a prefix from the dictionary entries below with one of the words in the box to make a new word, according to the definition.

line	clockwise	estimate	look	weight
wear	social	charge	freeze	

over- /əʊvəʳ/ **1** too much: *overpopular* | *overcooked cabbage* **2** above; beyond; across: *overhanging branches* | *the overland route* (= not by sea or air) **3** outer; covering: *an overcoat* **4** additional: *working overtime* (= beyond the usual time)

anti- /æntaɪ, æntɪ/ **1** opposed to; against: *antinuclear* (= opposing the use of atomic weapons and power) **2** opposite of: an *anticlimax* (= an unexciting ending instead of the expected CLIMAX)| *antimatter* (= made of material completely opposite in kind to the ordinary material in the universe) **3** acting to prevent the stated thing: *antiseptic* (= to stop bacteria)

under- /ʌndəʳ/ **1** too little: *underdevelopment* | *undercooked cabbage* **2** going underneath: *an underpass* **3** inner; beneath others: *undergarments* **4** less important or lower in rank: *a head gardener and three undergardeners*

1 (n): the clothes worn next to the body beneath other clothing
underwear

2 (adj): not showing concern for other people
....

3 (adj): weighing too little
....

4 (v): to guess at too low a value
....

5 (adv): in the opposite direction to the movement of a clock
....

6 (v): to ask too high a price for
....

7 (n): chemical substance used to stop water from freezing (esp. in cars)
....

8 (v): to stress or emphasise
....

9 (v): to not notice, to miss
....

Unit 27

GRAMMAR: the gerund (*-ing* form) after prepositions

1 **Complete the advertisement by choosing a preposition from the box and changing the form of the verb in brackets.**

by	from	without	instead of	after
before				

TV VISION HIRE

We are a company with a difference!

Our aim is to stop you [1]. *from wasting*.. (waste) your money!

[2]............................. (spend) money on an expensive new television set every few years, you can simply rent one from us at a fraction of the price. You can keep up with your neighbours [3] .... (change) your set for a newer model just as often as you like. And you get all this [4] ....(have to pay) any tiresome and expensive repair bills if your set goes wrong!

[5] .... (make) a final decision, why not pay us a visit at one of our showrooms in your area and have a look at some of the amazing sets we have for you to rent. If, [6] .... (talk) to one of our staff, you are still uncertain, we will give you a FREE SET for a one-month trial period.

Call us now on 081 992 5532 for more details.

VOCABULARY: machines and gadgets

2 **Use the pictures to complete the nine words below and find the name of another gadget in column 10.**

10

1 P O R T A B L E T E L E V I S I O N
2 C H
3 U T
4 I C
5 O S
6 R E
7 S O
8 O N
9 I O

1

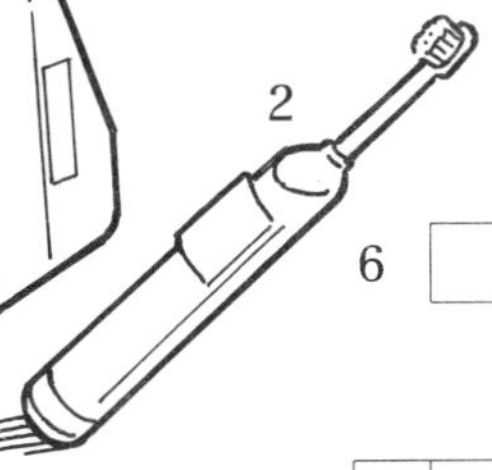
2

3

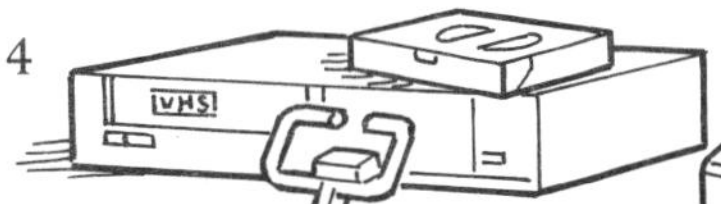
4

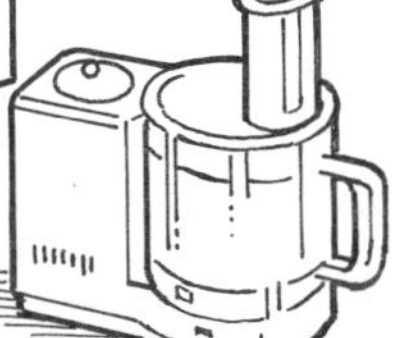
5

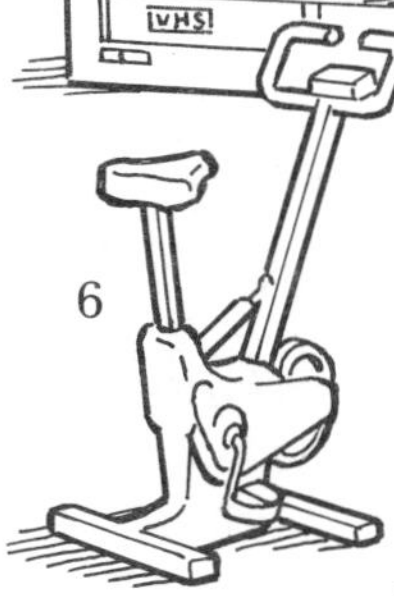
6

7

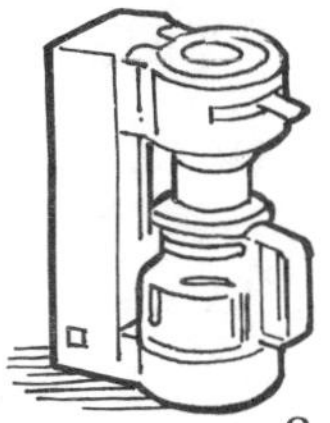
8

9

VOCABULARY: noun suffixes

3 **Complete the table.**

Verb	Noun (person or machine) (*-er/-or*)	Abstract noun (*-ion/-ment/-ing*)
simulate	*simulator*	*simulation*
examine	....	....
generate	....	....
develop	....	....
train	....	....
record	....	....
extract	....	....

Unit 28

GRAMMAR: future continuous

1 Read about the four people and make sentences about their hopes and their expectations for the future.

1 James has just finished a modelling course.
- model clothes for *Vogue*
- make coffee commercials on television

I hope I'll be modelling clothes for Vogue but I expect I'll be ....

....

2 Sue-Ann has just spent three years at drama school.
- act in a West End musical
- work in a hotel in Brighton

....

....

....

3 Paul has just been on a two-year intensive tennis course in Florida.
- play in international tournaments
- coach children at school

....

....

....

4 Melanie has completed a year's apprenticeship on a local newspaper.
- work as a foreign correspondent
- answer problem letters in a women's magazine

....

....

....

LISTENING

2 Listen to an extract from the news and answer the questions.

1 What event will be taking place tomorrow?

....

....

2 Where?

....

3 How will many fans be spending the night?

....

....

4 How will the organisers be separating the fans?

....

....

5 What will the police be doing?

....

6 What do the English fans want to know?

....

7 Why is this uncertain?

....

....

COMMUNICATION: conversational responses

3 **Choose the correct response from the box to complete the dialogue.**

I don't expect so.	I'm afraid not.	I expect so.
Of course not.	I don't think so.	I hope not.

JOE: It's not three thirty yet, is it?

TIM: [1]*I hope not.* I've got an appointment at three thirty. No, it's just after three.

JOE: Good. I've got to phone Angela. Have you got 10p change for the payphone?

TIM: Let's see. No, [2]........................ Sorry. Why don't you try the café?

JOE: Do you think they'd change a ten pound note?

TIM: [3]........................ They usually don't mind.

JOE: But it's after three o'clock. Won't it be closed by now?

TIM: [4]........................ They normally stay open all afternoon.

JOE: Oh great. Listen, would you mind keeping an eye on my bag?

TIM: [5]........................

JOE: Thanks. I'll be back in a moment.
(A few moments later).
O.K., I've got it. Is anybody using the payphone now?

TIM: [6]........................ It's been out of order for three weeks!

JOE: Thanks for telling me!

ORAL EXERCISES

4 **Make conversational responses.**

T: Will you be working late tonight? (✓ afraid)
S: *I'm afraid so.*
T: We're not going to be late, are we? (X think)
S: *I don't think so.*
T: Is your cold any better today? (X afraid)
S: *I'm afraid not.*

1 Will you be working late tonight? (✓ afraid)
2 We're not going to be late, are we? (X think)
3 Is your cold any better today? (X afraid)
4 I wonder if the weather will clear up by tomorrow. (✓ hope)
5 Have you finished with that book yet? (X afraid)
6 Will Simon be bringing that dreadful friend of his? (X hope)
7 Does the film start at nine? (✓ expect)
8 Is it February 15th today? (✓ think)

WRITING: a formal letter about future arrangements

5 **Rewrite the letter in your notebook, correcting the mistakes which are circled. Use the symbols in the margin as a guide. (See page 8 for the marking key.)**

Chaussee de Vleurgat 231
1050 Paris
France ^

Mr T. Tsuji
1069-1 Saijo-higashi
Saijocho Higashi Hiroshima 724

Dear Mr Tsuji,

Thank you for your letter. I (write) to tell you my travel arrangements for my trip to Tokyo on (monday july 1st) I will (arrive to) Narita Airport at 1425 on flight number JAL325.I hope the flight will be (in time). — t, p, gr, exp

I'm 1.85 tall. When I arrive, I (am wearing) a beige raincoat and (carry) a black briefcase. My friends tell me that the weather is fine in Tokyo at this time of year.I hope (yes!) — t, t, exp

I look forward to (meet) you. — gr

Yours (sincerly,) — sp

Jean-Claude Trudeau
Jean-Claude Trudeau

Now write a similar letter to Mr Trudeau using the following flight information. Don't forget to say what you look like and what you will be wearing.

AIR FRANCE	AF543		confirmed
	Tues 5 Apr		
Depart	London (Heathrow)	13.05	
Arrive	Paris (Charles de Gaulle)	15.50	

Unit 29

LISTENING: adverbs describing speech

1 **Match the appropriate adverb/adverbial phrase from the box with the sentences on the tape.**

gently politely in a shocked voice excitedly urgently nervously impatiently

1 *impatiently*
2 ...
3 ...
4 ...
5 ...
6 ...
7 ...

GRAMMAR: punctuation

2 **Rewrite the following conversation in your notebook, inserting the correct punctuation.**

Have you got it Fred whispered what do you mean replied Sam angrily of course I've got it but you don't seem to be carrying anything Fred protested so I thought . . . Well, you thought wrong didn't you Sam snapped I've got it in my pocket he pulled out a small package about the size of a matchbox now Sam whispered give this to Bobo with this message from the boss the boss says . . . He hesitated as he tried to recall the exact words happy birthday

VOCABULARY: crossword

3 **Complete the crossword.**

ACROSS
1 The complete circular path of an electric current (7)
4 Ask for money (3)
6 Could you give ... a lift? (2)
7 Fail to win (4)
9 Not many (3)
11 Rub out (5)
12 Once more (5)
13 You ought to ... the Museum of Modern Art in New York. (5)
14 We get ... very well together.(2)
16 Depressed (3)
17 Midday (4)
18 Machine which does work of a human being (5)
19 Instrument for writing (3)
20 Not second-hand (3)

DOWN
1 The colour and skin texture of someone's face (10)
2 Sympathy for the suffering of others (10)
3 Not well (3)
4 Meat from a cow (4)
5 To increase in size (4)
8 If you are ill, you might have this in hospital (10)
10 To calculate or judge the value or degree of (10)
15 Opposite of *then* (3)
16 A couple's daughter's husband is their ...-in-law
18 Prefix meaning 'to repeat or do again' (2)

Unit 30

GRAMMAR: *much/a bit* + comparative adjective + *than/not as ... as*

1 **Complete the sentences using the information about the televisions from the chart. Use the modifiers *much, a bit* and *not as ... as* in your sentences.**

	PHILIPS	SONY	FINLUX	FERGUSON
Price (to buy)	£300	£350	£450	£600
Screen size	51cm	53cm	59cm	220cm
Facilities	Nicam Stereo sound	Nicam Stereo sound Teletext	Nicam Stereo Sound Teletext On screen graphics	Wide screen Teletext
Rental	£18.99 a month	£19.49 a month	£21.49 a month	£25.99 a month

1 The Ferguson is *much more expensive to buy than* the Philips. (expensive to buy)
2 The Finlux is .... the Ferguson. (expensive to buy)
3 The screen on the Sony is .... the screen on the Philips. (large)
4 The screen on the Ferguson is .... the screen on the Philips. (large)
5 The Finlux is .... the Sony. (sophisticated)
6 The Ferguson is .... the Finlux. (sophisticated)
7 The Philips is .... the Sony. (cheap to rent)
8 The Finlux is .... the Sony. (cheap to rent)

LISTENING

2 **Brian is a foreign correspondent who has been working in Africa. He is now back at his news desk in London. Listen to his conversation with another journalist and make notes under the headings.**

Advantages of being a foreign correspondent:

1 ....
2 ....
3 ....
4 ....

Advantages of working on the news desk in London:

1 ....
2 ....
3 ....

READING

3 **Read the article in which Wen-Ling, an author, talks about her brother, Chien-Kuo.**

FAMILY *values*

Wen-Ling, an author, talks about her brother, Chien-Kuo

'We have a saying in China that "the emperor must love the eldest son but the ordinary person must love the youngest son." Chien-Kuo was the youngest son for six years and he was easy to love. He's so good-natured. Chien-Kuo has tremendous strength of character. He's an optimist and has a great capacity for laughter. I'm much more serious and agonise over things. Sometimes I'm full of self-doubt so I ring Chien-Kuo and ask him, "Did I say the right thing at dinner?" Invariably his answer will be teasing. He'll say, "For God's sake, what are you worrying about?"

My brother is an excellent writer but right now he can't work at what he enjoys most. His special interests are politics and economics - subjects I find quite difficult. I'm much more interested in the human face of a story.

My brother has had a tough life. When he was younger, other kids used to bully him, but he always finds the resources to cope with circumstances. I'm the impatient one, always looking for a way out of situations. When I was sent to the country I couldn't wait to find a way back to the town and the factory. I admire the way my brother just gets on with life. The more I get to know Chien-Kuo, the more I love him.'

Compare Wen-Ling and her brother in the following respects:

1 HUMOUR

Compared with her brother, Wen-Ling is much more serious.

or

Chien-Kuo is more likely to laugh at things than his sister.

2 CONFIDENCE

3 INTEREST IN POLITICS AND ECONOMICS

4 INTEREST IN PEOPLE

5 PATIENCE

GRAMMAR: *more/less* + adjectival phrase

4 **Make sentences to compare young people nowadays to young people fifty years ago. When there is a plus sign (+), use *more* and the adjectival phrase; when there is a minus sign (−), use *less* and the adjectival phrase.**

Young people today compared to fifty years ago:

1 + LIKELY TO	spend money on CDs
2 − INTERESTED IN	buy single records
3 + WORRIED ABOUT	get a job
4 − LIKELY TO	suffer from ill health
5 + ABLE TO	express their feelings
6 + INTERESTED IN	travel abroad

1 *Young people today are more likely to spend money on CDs.*

2 *They are less interested in*

3

4

5

6

PROGRESS TEST UNITS 26–30

1 Complete each sentence so that it means the same as the preceding sentence.

1 His sound system isn't as good as mine.
My ....
....

2 Haven't you got any larger sweaters?
Is this ....
....

3 Jill plays the piano better than Simon.
Simon is not ....
....

4 Prices in the USA are cheap compared to Britain at the moment.
Prices in the USA are much ....
....

5 Sweden is more likely to win the Cup than Norway.
Norway ....
....

6 If you cut down on salt, you'll reduce the risk of heart disease.
By ....
....

7 You shouldn't argue with her. You should try to talk things over.
Instead of ....
....

8 Normally we go abroad for our holiday but not this year.
I'm afraid we won't ....
....

2 Complete the sentences with the correct form of the word in capital letters.

1 Don't get an electric tin opener. They're
.... USE

2 We've got to try and be more .... over the use of water. ECONOMY

3 There is a massive .... on jeans in the sale at the moment. REDUCE

4 Sadly, the doctors say the disease is
.... CURE

5 They've made an amazing archaeological
.... in the Lebanon. DISCOVER

6 They live in a village in Wales with a
completely .... name. PRONOUNCE

7 It was one of the most .... evenings we've had for a long time. ENJOY

8 What's the .... of me getting a work permit? LIKELY

3 Circle A, B, or C to indicate the word or phrase which best completes each sentence.

1 John is on a business ... to Hong Kong.
A trip B travel C excursion D journey

2 There has been a big ... in the number of children hurt on the roads this year.
A lift B rise C raise D arise

3 She wants to ... her visa for another six months.
A increase B expand C extend D lengthen

4 After the accident, she suffered a complete ... of memory.
A lack B shortage C loss D decrease

5 Will we have a ... to visit the Houses of Parliament?
A hope B occasion C event D chance

6 We need to take some ... advice on this matter.
A monetary B financial C economical D economic

7 Don't open the oven. You might ... the cake.
A spoil B harm C hurt D destroy

8 The film was boring at first but it began to pick ... later on.
A out B on C up D at

Unit 31

VOCABULARY: nouns and adjectives

1 **Make adjectives from the nouns in the left-hand column.**

Noun	Adjective
1 hill	hilly
2 mountain	....
3 agriculture	....
4 coast	....
5 commerce	....
6 industry	....
7 history	....
8 culture	....

VOCABULARY: types of towns

2 **Use the pictures to write a sentence describing the following cities, towns and villages.**

CITIES

1 Rouen, France

Rouen is a cathedral city in France.

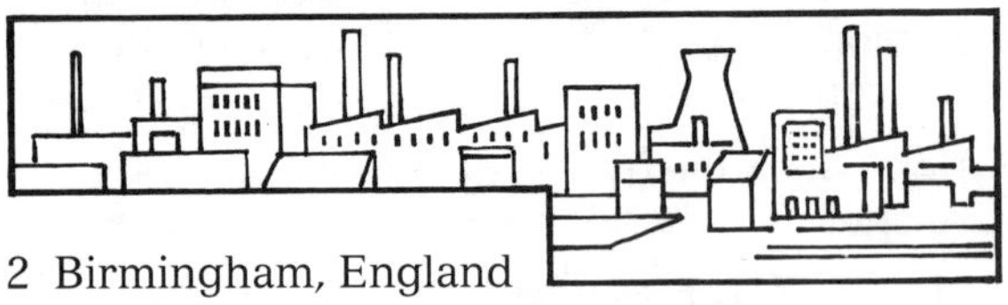

2 Birmingham, England

....

3 Washington DC, USA

....

TOWNS

4 Uppsala, Sweden

....

5 Newmarket, England

....

6 Rimini, Italy

....

VILLAGES

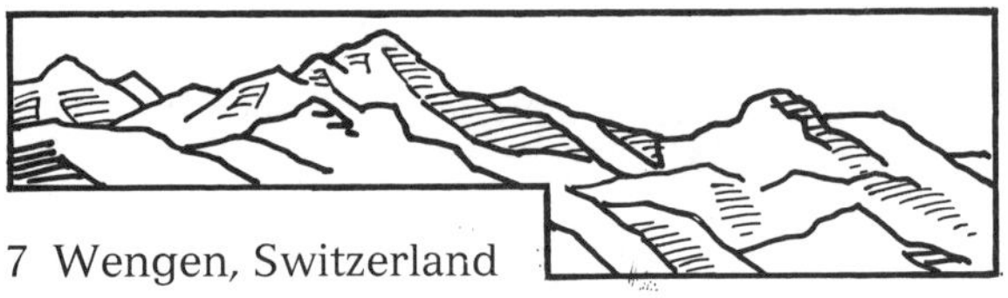

7 Wengen, Switzerland

....

8 Fuzeta, Portugal

....

LISTENING

3 **A couple have invited a friend round to see some slides of their 'Round the World in Eight Days' holiday. Listen to the conversation and write the places that they went to each day.**

Day 1: USA (New York)	Day 5: ....
Day 2:	Day 6: ....
Day 3:	Day 7: ....
Day 4:	Day 8: ....

VOCABULARY: common mistakes

4 **Complete the letter choosing the correct word in italics.**

Dear Cathy,

We are really looking forward to your 1*stay/visit* to Holland. The best 2*possible/suitable* time for us would be in two weeks' time when we've both got a week off, but there are other 3*opportunities/possibilities*, like early May or June, for instance. By the way, we lead a very quiet 4*life/lives* here. You won't need to bring very much money, just enough to buy a few 5*curiosities/souvenirs* at the end of your holiday. Did I tell you, John has now bought a Land Rover?

It's still a bit of a 6*news/novelty* so there's a 7*chance/opportunity* he'll drive to Schipol and pick you up from the airport. Let us know your dates when you can.

Love,

Amanda

P.S. Just out of 8*novelty/curiosity*, what does your new boyfriend actually do for a 9*living/work*?

GRAMMAR: definite and zero article with place names

5 **Complete this description of the city of Prague by filling in the definite article where necessary.**

Prague, 1 ...the... romantic capital of the Czech Republic, is acknowledged to be one of 2......... most imposing and beautiful cities in 3......... Europe.

4......... city is situated on either side of 5......... River Vlatva, which is spanned by many fine bridges, including 6......... Charles Bridge. Prague is dominated by 7......... Hradcany Castle, which includes within its walls 8......... Cathedral of St. Vitus. For many centuries this castle was 9......... home of the Bohemian kings and is now 10......... residence of 11......... President of the Republic.

12......... Wenceslas Square, in 13......... centre of Prague, is 14......... heart of the city. Here you will find 15......... National Museum which houses a remarkable collection of 16......... natural history and geological exhibits.

Music-lovers will want to visit 17......... Dvořák museum and the house in 18......... Lazenska Street where Ludwig van Beethoven lived.

Unit 32

GRAMMAR: mixed passive forms

1 Transform the following active sentences into passive sentences.

1 Nobody will know the result of the election until late tonight.
The result of the election will not be known until late tonight.

2 The hotel staff clean the rooms thoroughly every day.

....

....

3 They have postponed the match until next Saturday.

....

....

4 They were raising money during the evening for charity.

....

....

5 Someone is repairing the video at this very moment.

....

....

6 They should have posted the parcel on Thursday.

....

....

7 They are going to redecorate the college during the holidays.

....

....

8 They discovered some Roman treasure in the middle of a cornfield in Sussex last week.

....

....

....

GRAMMAR: passive infinitive, gerund and modals

2 Complete the article with the correct form of the passive using the verbs in brackets.

POACHING IN Africa

Last month more rhinos were murdered by poachers in Africa. The horns were cut off and the bodies left where they fell.

There is no doubt now that putting a fence around suitable areas to keep out poachers is the only way the rhinos 1 *can be protected* (can/protect). A 200 kilometre boundary has now been cleared in Kenya and is ready for electric fences 2.......................... (erect). Accommodation for the wardens has already been built and a water powered generator is in the process of 3..................................(construct).

The second phase of this fencing project is now ready to begin. The fence posts 4.................................. (can/obtain) in Kenya, but wire 5 ....(have to/buy) from Europe. We cannot allow the project 6.. (abandon) at this stage so we are asking for your help to raise the necessary funds.

When this project began three years ago it seemed impossibly expensive, but there is now some hope that it 7.................................. (may/achieve). Without these sanctuaries 8 .... completely ....(fence), there is still the danger of some rhinos wandering out of the sanctuaries and 9 .... (kill) by poachers.

We are appealing for your help with these important projects. The future of the rhino in Kenya is in our hands. Please help us ensure their survival.

WAA WORLD ANIMAL AID

LISTENING

3 **Listen to some news items. Note down the details of each item under the headings below.**

	Incident 1
WHAT?	hurricane
WHERE?	....
WHEN?	....
DETAILS:	....

	Incident 2
WHAT?	....
WHERE?	....
WHEN?	....
DETAILS:	....

	Incident 3
WHAT?	....
WHERE?	....
WHEN?	....
DETAILS:	....

WRITING

4 **Use the notes below to reconstruct a story for a newspaper article.**

DRAMATIC MINE RESCUE

- Denver, Colorado. 2-year-old Mindy Shiner rescued after being trapped in 30cm diameter disused mine shaft
- Rescue started after child's cries heard by passing motorist
- While rescue taking place, Mindy kept alive by air tube and water pipe
- Reunited last night with family
- Examined by doctors/described as "being quite unharmed" after her ordeal

VOCABULARY: mixed words

5 **Write these verbs next to their correct definitions.**

hamper	devastate	boycott	migrate
assassinate	torture	threaten	imprison
bully	contaminate		

1 threaten.........: to be a danger to; seem likely to harm, spoil, ruin

2 ....: to destroy completely (a city, area of land) so that nothing useful or valuable remains

3 ....: to cause difficulty in movement or activity

4 ....: to make impure or bad by mixing impure, dirty or poisonous matter

5 ....: to travel regularly from one part of the world to another, according to the seasons of the year

6 ....: to put in a prison or keep in a place or state which one is not free to leave

7 ....: to murder (a ruler, politician, or other important person)

8 ....: to refuse to do business with, attend, or take part in, as a way of showing disapproval and opposition

9 ....: to cause great pain or suffering in order to force someone to give information

10 ....: to intentionally frighten or hurt weaker people

Unit 33

COMMUNICATION: speculation

1 Write a number 1, 2 or 3 next to each sentence according to its meaning.

1 = 99% unlikely or improbable
2 = possible
3 = probable or 99% certain

	Number
1 I'm sure John's been held up in a traffic jam.	3
2 He said he did the journey in three hours! That's impossible.	
3 Perhaps Jo's decided to have an early night.	
4 I'm sure the train left early.	
5 That wasn't an elephant, surely! It was too small.	
6 It's highly likely you dropped the envelope as you were running for the bus.	
7 There's a chance that one of our employees has double-booked your ticket.	
8 I'm sure they decided to take the train after all.	
9 Maybe they missed the turning.	

2 Now write each sentence again using *can't have*, *might have* or *must have* and a verb in the past participle.

1 John must have been held up in a traffic jam.

2 ....

3 ....

4 ....

5 ....

6 ....

7 ....

8 ....

9 ....

3 Complete the dialogue with the correct form (simple or continuous) of the modals in the past.

PETER: Hi, Louise! I've been trying to get in touch with you all week.

LOUISE: Really?

PETER: Yes, first I tried to phone you on Monday evening. I suppose it was about 7.30.

LOUISE: Oh, I 1 must have already left (must/already/leave) for the cinema.

PETER: Then on Tuesday evening I phoned at about six o'clock.

LOUISE: I 2 .... (might/work late). I usually do on a Tuesday.

PETER: Then I tried again on Wednesday, at about ten o'clock in the evening.

LOUISE: Really? I suppose I 3 .... (might/already/go to bed). I had an early night, I think, on Wednesday.

PETER: Then I tried on Thursday evening around eight o'clock.

LOUISE: I 4 .... (must/shop). It's late night shopping on Thursday.

PETER: Then last night I tried several times but still no luck!

LOUISE: I think I 5 .... (might/have) a shower.

PETER: What! For four hours! You 6 .... (can't/be) in the shower all evening! I get the feeling you're trying to avoid me, Louise.

LOUISE: Whatever gave you that idea?

ORAL EXERCISES

4 **Draw possible conclusions.**

T: He was found wandering around the house at three in the morning. (he/sleepwalk)
S: *He might have been sleepwalking.*

1 He was found wandering around the house at three in the morning. (he/sleepwalk)
2 I don't know who she was talking to for so long. (she/phone her boyfriend)
3 Why did you tell me to turn down the music? (the neighbours/try to sleep)
4 There was a strange sound outside the sitting room window last night. (someone/try to break in)
5 I phoned her but her number was engaged. (she/try to phone you)
6 You weren't in when I called yesterday. (I/sit in the garden)

5 **Draw definite conclusions.**

T: I couldn't see the little boy anywhere. (he/hide)
S: *He must have been hiding.*
T: She suddenly forgot what she was saying. (she/concentrate)
S: *She can't have been concentrating.*

1 I couldn't see the little boy anywhere. (he/hide)
2 She suddenly forgot what she was saying. (she/concentrate)
3 Sally wasn't home when I called. (she/fetch the children)
4 He came last in the race. (he/try)
5 The man was stopped in his car by the police. (he/drink and drive)
6 I didn't hear the announcement at all. (you/doze)
7 Don't you remember I said we'd be late? (I/listen)
8 Her eyes were red and puffy. (she/cry)
9 She got burnt on the first day on the beach! (she/wear any suntan lotion)
10 The man couldn't fix the tap in the end. (he/use the right tools)

VOCABULARY: crossword

6 **Complete the crossword.**

ACROSS
2 Nocturnal animals found in Britain (7)
5 Opposite of *minor* (5)
6 To cover a present with paper (4)
8 Part of verb *to be* (2)
10 Past tense of *to eat* (3)
11 Very unusual (4)
13 I must buy some new clothes. I've got nothing to . . . (4)
15 Useful auxiliary verb in English (2)
17 To change the colour of something, e.g. hair (3)
19 A cooked meat (3)
21 A sharp-edged weapon (3)
22 A mass of ice at the top of a mountain (7)
25 An affirmative answer (3)
26 Examined closely (7)

DOWN
1 Body decoration (6)
2 A curved weapon for shooting 3 down (3)
3 A long, thin, pointed weapon (3)
4 The sound that a lion makes (4)
7 To speak, often silently, to a god (4)
9 Object pronoun (2)
12 Region (4)
14 Short for *Edward* (2)
15 You do this with a spade. (3)
16 The house . . . south. (5)
18 I haven't . . . from John for ages. (5)
19 Dry grass (3)
20 Not as thick as fog (4)
24 Colour of double-decker buses in London (3)

Unit 34

1 **Read the following article about Christopher Columbus and list the information about him in your notebook under the two headings below.**

Traditional view

1 *Columbus was the first European to discover America.*

Alternative view

1 *The Vikings got to America first. Codfishers from Bristol discovered Newfoundland in the 1480s.*

CHRISTOPHER COLUMBUS
Fact or Fallacy?

The 500th anniversary of the landing of Christopher Columbus in the New World was celebrated on October 12th 1992. But many historians today are disputing certain details of the conventional Columbus story.

- Columbus is said to have been the first European to reach America but this is now widely disputed. There is plenty of evidence to show that the Vikings got there first. It is also thought that cod-fishers from Bristol in the west of England stumbled on Newfoundland in the 1480s. They kept their discovery a secret because they did not want anyone else to find out about their cod-fishing grounds.
- It is often claimed that Columbus was the first person to sight land on his first voyage to the New World. Indeed, a huge prize had been promised to the first sailor to do so. On his return to Europe, Columbus claimed this for himself and the sailor who had in fact first sighted land was cheated of his prize.
- It is said that Columbus had to persuade people that the earth was not flat. Most educated people knew that already.
- Columbus is frequently described in history books as a great and noble explorer. However, he is seen by some as a ruthless imperialist, responsible for the slavery and destruction of America's native tribes. Columbus described the first American Indians he met as 'so much our friends that it is a marvel'. But his rule in Hispaniola prompted thousands of Indians to commit suicide.
- Contrary to what people think, Columbus was not left to die in poverty; he just died in obscurity.

GRAMMAR: *It is said that . . . / . . . is/are said to have . . .*

2 **Rephrase these sentences with an appropriate passive construction using the words in italics. Begin with the words given in brackets.**

1 People *say* that Watling Island in the Bahamas was Columbus' first port of call. (It ...)

It is said that Watling Island in the Bahamas was Columbus' first port of call.

2 People *think* that a hundred thousand of the population of Hispaniola died within two years of Columbus' arrival. (A hundred thousand ...)

A hundred thousand of the population of Hispaniola are thought to have died within two years of Columbus' arrival.

3 The common *belief* is that Columbus landed first in the Bahamas. (Columbus ...)

4 Some people *think* that Columbus was an imperialist. (It ...)

5 People *say* that Columbus' real name was Cristobal Colon. (Columbus' real ...)

6 A lot of people *think* that Columbus died in poverty. (It ...)

Unit 35

READING

1 **Put the paragraphs in order to form an account of 'The American Indians' Fight for Survival'.**

A

At first the American Indians tried to drive the white newcomers away. Soon they saw that this was impossible so they made an agreement with the government in Washington to give up large areas of land for white farmers to settle on. In return, the government promised to leave the American Indians in peace.

B

The American army encouraged the killing of the buffalo. They saw it as a way of ending the American Indian resistance to the occupation of their land. Soon the government decided to send an army to force the American Indians off their land and onto 'reservations' - dry, rocky areas that nobody wanted.

C

The American Indians lived peacefully in this way for many years until the 1840s, when wagon trains began to cross the Great Plains. The American Indians usually let them pass without trouble. Then the railroads came carrying white people who stayed on the plains and began to cultivate them.

D

The American Indians did not want to be on the reservations and fought back. One of their best known leaders was Sitting Bull of the Sioux tribe. They won their best victory at the Battle of Little Big Horn in 1876. However, in the end the American army was too large and too powerful for the Sioux. With the buffalo gone, the Sioux surrendered.

E

Many hundreds of years ago, the American Indians inhabited the Great Plains in the American West. Tribes, like the Sioux, lived by hunting buffalo. In the early part of the nineteenth century approximately twelve million buffalo wandered the Great Plains. They provided the Sioux with everything they needed - food, clothing, tools and homes.

F

However, it was clear that the government were not going to keep their promise. In the years that followed, the farmers took more and more of their land and the buffalo began to disappear. What is more, white hunters were shooting the buffalo in thousands. In two years beteen 1872 and 1874 the hunters almost completely destroyed the great herds.

1 [E] 2 [ ] 3 [ ] 4 [ ] 5 [ ] 6 [ ]

2 **Read the text and answer *True* or *False*.**

1 The Sioux tribes used to live on the Great Plains many hundreds of years ago. [T]

2 The buffalo were important for the survival of the Sioux. [ ]

3 The American Indians began to protest when the white people began to settle on the land. [ ]

4 In the end the government agreed to let the American Indians have their land back. [ ]

5 White hunters began to kill the buffalo. [ ]

6 The government were shocked when they heard that the buffalo were being killed by the white hunters. [ ]

7 The American Indians were pleased to move to the special reservations. [ ]

8 The American Indians were defeated at the Battle of Little Big Horn. [ ]

9 In the end all the buffalo disappeared and the Sioux gave up their struggle. [ ]

WRITING

3 **Correct the statements in Exercise 2 which are false. Then use the nine statements as a basis for a summary of 'The American Indians' Fight for Survival'.**

Start like this:

Many hundreds of years ago, the Sioux tribe used to live ... They used to hunt ..., which were important for their survival. When the first wagon trains ...

GRAMMAR: prepositions and relative pronouns

4 **Combine the pairs of sentences with a preposition and a relative pronoun.**

1 Medicine is perhaps the most important of all sciences. Progress has been very rapid in this science.

Medicine, in which progress has been very rapid, is perhaps the most important of all sciences.

2 Mozart was a brilliant composer. Many books have been written about him.

....

....

....

3 The woman is my neighbour. I heard the story from her.

....

....

4 The environmental issue is becoming more important. I spoke about it yesterday.

....

....

....

5 The article was written by a friend of mine. Your name was mentioned in it.

....

....

....

....

GRAMMAR: omission of object relative pronouns

5 **Write the following sentences in informal spoken English by omitting the relative pronoun and placing the preposition at the end of the relative clause.**

1 The man to whom you were talking was Sally's father.

The man you were talking to was Sally's father.

2 The road along which you drove this evening has now been closed.

....

....

3 The person with whom I usually play badminton has broken her wrist.

....

....

4 The house in which I was born has now been demolished.

....

....

5 The apartment from which she moved was quite dark and dingy.

....

....

6 The time at which we were supposed to arrive was six o'clock.

....

....

7 Caroline is someone with whom I have nothing in common.

....

....

8 My assistant is someone in whom I have the greatest confidence.

....

....

PROGRESS TEST UNITS 31–35

1 Complete each sentence so that it means the same as the preceding sentence.

1 The rain has destroyed all the crops.

All the crops ....

....

2 The belief is that the woman was murdered.

The woman ....

....

3 Somone should tell his parents as soon as possible.

His parents ....

....

4 If you're caught drinking and driving, it's a serious offence.

Being ....

....

5 Perhaps he dropped his wallet in the street.

He might ....

....

6 The likelihood is that she caught the early ferry.

She must ....

....

7 I don't believe they left the restaurant without paying.

They can't ....

....

8 The man I was talking to was my Italian singing teacher.

The man to ....

....

2 Complete the sentences with the correct form of the word in capital letters.

1 Don't be fooled by him. Appearances can be very .... DECEIVE

2 The oil spill caused massive .... in the area. POLLUTE

3 You need to .... your insurance company within forty-eight hours. NOTE

4 He felt that the new assistant was a .... to his authority. THREATEN

5 The trouble is, he's completely .... when it comes to punctuality. RELY

6 A lot of good .... land is being turned into golf courses. AGRICULTURE

7 There's no need to worry .... about it. DUE

8 .... issues will be the main theme at the conference. ENVIRONMENT

3 Circle A, B or C to indicate the word or phrase which best completes each sentence.

1 We enjoyed our ... with our relatives in Vancouver immensely.
A visit B stay C rest D trip

2 The food processor was a great ... at first but it soon wore off.
A novelty B souvenir C curiosity D invention

3 When it comes to money, she takes ... her father.
A off B in C to D after

4 People are refusing to put their ... in the government any more.
A trust B belief C hope D confidence

5 Overpopulation is a very ... subject at the moment.
A current B topical C contemporary D actual

6 I'm not sure of the best route to Oxford, but there are several ... .
A chances B opportunities C examples D possibilities

7 It's better not to drink the water. It may be slightly ... .
A poisoned B infected C contaminated D damaged

8 The club had to close because I was the ... member!
A only B lonely C alone D solitary

Unit 36

COMMUNICATION: criticising people

1 Look at the following situation.

Sarah shares a flat with her younger brother, Tom. She is irritated because he continually:
- uses her walkman.
- borrows money from her.
- watches horror videos.
- uses her hair gel.

What's more, he:
- never does the washing-up.
- plays his guitar at two in the morning.
- never listens to what she says.
- hangs about the flat when her friends come round to visit.

Imagine you are Sarah. Write sentences to express your irritation at each of the bad habits above.

1 *You're always using my walkman!*
2 *You* ....
3 ....
4 ....
5 *I wish you would do the washing-up occasionally.*
6 *I wish* ....
....
7 ....
....
8 ....
....

ORAL EXERCISES

2 Criticise habits.

T: Anna broke a cup this morning.
S: *She's always breaking cups!*

1 Anna broke a cup this morning.
2 Then she cut herself with the bread knife.
3 Then Tim lost his schoolbag.
4 And he missed his train.
5 And Harry got into trouble with his teacher.
6 And then I watched *Neighbours* on TV.

3 Express irritation.

T: Mr Sanderson said could you type this letter? (write more legibly)
S: *I wish he'd write more legibly.*

1 Mr Sanderson said could you type this letter? (write more legibly)
2 John says it'll be another half an hour before he's ready. (hurry up)
3 Sarah's going out with Tom again this evening. (not/spend so much time with him)
4 We got this letter from the council this morning. (express themselves more clearly)
5 Dave's coming to stay for three weeks. (you/not/tell me things at the last minute)
6 Penny isn't sure if she's going to come on Saturday. (make her mind up)

4 Criticise past actions.

T: Why didn't you tell me?
S: *You might have told me!*

1 Why didn't you tell me?
2 Why didn't she write?
3 Why didn't he pay the bill?
4 I was a bit upset that they didn't lend a hand.
5 I can't understand why he didn't offer us a lift.
6 Why didn't you ask me first?

PHRASAL VERBS AND IDIOMS: *do*

5 Circle the word in the group which <u>cannot</u> follow the phrasal verb or idiom with *do*.

1 do: a) the washing b) one's best (c) a mistake
2 do up: a) a coat b) your socks c) the house
3 do with: a) a cup of tea b) a stomachache c) a haircut
4 do without: a) coffee b) his help c) the floor
5 do away with: a) air b) trade unions c) tax

Unit 37

GRAMMAR: inversion after negative adverb: *no sooner*

1 Combine the two sentences using *No sooner.*

1 I left the house. It started to rain.
No sooner had I left the house than it started to rain.

2 We finished our meal. The waiter presented us with the bill.
....

3 Nick dropped off to sleep. The alarm clock rang.
....

4 Jan got home. She realised she'd forgotten her dentist's appointment.
....

5 She decided to hand in her notice. She was offered a pay rise.
....

6 I put the baby to bed. She started to cry.
....

GRAMMAR: inversion after negative adverb: *not only*

2 Rephrase what the two people say in conversation, using *not only* and *also.*

1 A: She's got a great voice, hasn't she?
B: Yes, and she writes her own songs.
Not only has she got a great voice, she also writes her own songs.

2 A: The job's very boring.
B: What's more, it's very badly paid.
....

3 A: Bob's very bright, isn't he?
B: Yes, and he's got a great sense of humour.
....

4 A: You know she had to take them out for a meal?
B: Yes, and I heard she had to find them a hotel as well.
....

5 A: You know we have to pack our bags the night before, don't you?
B: Yes and we have to get up at half past four the next morning to catch the train!
....

6 A: John Barnes scored three goals in the Cup Final.
B: I know, and he was voted top player of the year.
....

GRAMMAR: reflexive pronouns

3 Complete the letter with the correct reflexive pronoun.

Dear Mum,
Today is a Red Letter Day! I washed and dressed 1 myself for the first time since the operation!
Yesterday being New Year's Eve, all the doctors, nurses and patients got together for a party. We all ate a lot and sang a lot and generally enjoyed 2.......... . One woman with a broken leg tried to dance and fell over. She didn't hurt 3.......... but it put me off trying!
Some of the patients on the ward performed a play they had written 4.........., which was very funny! We nearly killed 5.......... laughing!
See you on Wednesday. Tell Dad to look after 6.......... when he goes skiing or he'll end up in hospital like me!

Unit 38

GRAMMAR: gerund or infinitive?

1 Complete the sentences with the correct form of the verb.

1 A: Do you want (go) to go .... out for something to eat?
B: No, I don't really feel like (eat) .... out.

2 A: I've decided (give up) ....
(watch television) ....
B: I've heard you say that before but you've never managed (give up) .... for more than a day!

3 A: The cat absolutely refuses (eat) .... that new brand of cat food you bought.
B: Well, we'll have to give it something else, then. There's no use (leave) .... it there if it's not going to eat it.
A: But I can't stand (waste) .... perfectly good cat food.

4 A: Have you succeeded in (persuade) .... Tina and John to come with us on holiday?
B: Not yet. There doesn't seem (be) .... much point in (invite) .... them until we're sure of the dates.

5 A: How are you enjoying (live) .... here?
B: It's O.K., but sometimes I can't help (feel) .... a bit homesick. At times I just feel like (get) .... on a plane and (fly) .... straight back home.

LISTENING

2 Listen to the conversation between a couple at an airport and the girl behind the check-in counter. Choose the correct answer.

1 The man is angry because
a) he can't find their tickets.
b) the flight is overbooked.
c) he has arrived late and their seats have been sold.

2 The girl says that the fault is
a) hers.
b) the couple's.
c) the airline's.

3 The couple had planned to
a) meet some friends in Manchester for lunch.
b) catch a connecting flight from Manchester at midday.
c) catch the 1.30 flight to Manchester.

4 The couple are offered
a) seats on the next available flight.
b) a free meal.
c) the use of a telephone.

5 The couple eventually agree to
a) go on the 11.30 flight to Manchester.
b) go on the 1.30 flight.
c) come back another day.

VOCABULARY: compound nouns

3 **Match the words from Column A with suitable words from Column B to make compound nouns.**

A	B
mountain	bag
country	path
sleeping	walk
walking	stick
search	rescue
	trip
	pass
	party

1 mountain path.... mountain ....

mountain .... mountain ....

2 country .... country ....

3 sleeping ....

4 walking .... walking ....

walking ....

5 search ....

GRAMMAR: revision of verbs of reporting

4 **Use the cues in brackets to report what the people involved in a mountain rescue incident actually said.**

1 'I've come to Nepal to work in a local hospital as part of my medical studies.' (James/explain)

James explained that.........................

....

....

....

2 'Why don't we attempt a more exciting route?' (Mark/suggest)

....

....

3 'Don't worry. I'll meet you in Kathmandu on December 25th.' (James/promise/Mark)

....

....

4 'Don't worry, Dad. I'll go out to Kathmandu and search for James.' (Joanne/offer)

....

....

5 'I think the best man to hire is Carl Harrison, an experienced mountaineer.' (The president of the Himalayan Research Association/ recommend)

....

....

....

6 'Why don't you consult a Buddhist lama?' (a girl at the airport/suggest/Joanne)

....

....

....

7 'I won't give up hope!' (Joanne/refuse)

....

....

8 'You will meet your brother again.' (the lama/ assure/Joanne)

....

....

9 'We have spotted a person who is alive.' (Colonel Pun/announce)

....

....

Unit 39

GRAMMAR: stressed auxiliaries

1 Make the following sentences more emphatic, either by adding an auxiliary to the verb in italics or by expanding the contracted auxiliary in italics.

1 You won't need an expensive encyclopaedia but *you'll* need a good dictionary.

You won't need an expensive encyclopaedia but you will need a good dictionary.

2 He didn't say he wasn't coming to the meeting but he *said* he'd be a bit late.

....

3 They're not having a big party but they*'re going out* with a few friends.

....

4 We didn't hear from him for a year although we *got* one or two postcards.

....

5 I'm not very keen on fish, though I *love* crab.

....

6 I didn't know she was going to have a baby but I *knew* that she was married.

....

GRAMMAR: cleft sentences

2 Make the second sentence more emphatic each time by using a cleft sentence.

1 Kate doesn't mind snakes or spiders. She doesn't like mice!

What she doesn't like is mice!

2 I've got the bread and butter. I've forgotten the cheese!

....

3 I can understand why you didn't reply to any of my letters. I don't understand why you lied to me.

....

4 He told me he'd had an accident while he was cooking. He didn't tell me that he'd burnt the kitchen table!

....

5 I know your address and telephone number. I don't know your last name!

....

6 I don't mind people criticising me. I can't stand people who do it behind my back.

....

GRAMMAR: adverb of emphasis: *that*

3 **Look at the pictures and complete the conversations, using *that* for emphasis and one of the adjectives from the box below.**

rich	ill	bad	tired	tight

1

MOTHER: Why don't you go to bed?

BOY: *I'm not that tired*............!

2

MAN 1: Why don't you go in and buy it?

MAN 2: ....!

3

WOMAN: Those trousers don't seem to fit you any more.

MAN: ....!

4

MAN: This is an awful film. Why don't we leave?

WOMAN: ....!

5

GIRL 1: Don't you think you should take the day off work?

GIRL 2: ....!

GRAMMAR: adverb of emphasis: *really*

4 **Make the sentences more emphatic by putting *really* in the appropriate place each time.**

1 I'm very pleased with the results.

I'm really very pleased with the results.

2 I think you should take a taxi home at this time of night.

....

....

3 It was stupid of me not to book seats in advance.

....

....

4 I was exhausted after all the travelling.

....

....

5 For a learner, he drives well.

....

WRITING: balancing phrases

5 **Use the notes in the chart to write sentences with the balancing phrases indicated.**

	TOPIC	OPINION/FACT	BALANCING OPINION/FACT
	At first sight . . . but in actual fact . . .		
1	Using a phone card	complicated	very simple
2	Learning to play the piano	easy	requires a lot of practice
3	Modelling	glamorous career	very stressful
	In theory . . . but in practice . . .		
4	Driving test	possible to pass it after a few lessons	takes at least ten
5	The sights of London	possible to see in a couple of days	need at least a week
6	President of the USA	anyone can become president	candidate has to be fairly rich
	It may be true that . . . but on the whole . . .		
7	Seat-belts	may not always work	they have saved thousands of lives
8	Number of fast food restaurants	on the increase	people are now more health-conscious
9	Some young people	lazy	most want to get a job

1 *At first sight using a phone card looks complicated but in actual fact it is very simple.*

2 ....

3 ....

4 *In theory it's possible to pass a driving test after only a few lessons but in practice it takes at least ten.*

5 ....

6 ....

7 *It may be true that seat-belts may not always work but on the whole they have saved thousands of lives.*

8 ....

9 ....

Unit 40

VOCABULARY: adjectives: degrees of intensity

1 Match the following adjectives with a stronger equivalent.

1 irritated	a) passionate
2 good	b) stunning
3 happy	c) devastated
4 upset	d) suicidal
5 affectionate	e) exasperated
6 frightened	f) dreary
7 bad	g) ecstatic
8 boring	h) petrified
9 attractive	i) fantastic
10 depressed	j) appalling

LISTENING

2 Listen to Jane, an actress who played Rita in a stage performance of the play *Educating Rita*, and tick the best answers.

1 Which of the following points does she think the play makes about education?

a) It feeds and nourishes. ☐

b) It is a waste of time. ☐

c) It can be threatening. ☐

d) It gives you a choice in life. ☐

e) It can help you choose which books to read. ☐

f) It makes you feel you want to sing about life. ☐

2 Why does she think it is such a popular play?

a) People can identify with the characters and story. ☐

b) It's not just a love story. ☐

c) People like the accents. ☐

d) It's funny. ☐

e) It's exciting. ☐

f) The characters are believable. ☐

READING: idioms to do with 'life'

3 Complete the paragraphs with a suitable idiom to do with *life*.

1
We've just been on a course on how to write a best-seller. It was great fun. There were all sorts of people there. There was a politician, a housewife, a painter, a window-cleaner, a bank manager and a teacher. In fact there were *people from all walks of life*..........

2
My brother found an old bicycle in a field last week. He cleaned it up, painted it, bought a new chain and generally gave it ....
....

3
Last Saturday Sam, a ten-year-old handicapped child, went with some school friends to an amusement park. He went on the Big Dipper, drove a dodgem car, had a pony ride, travelled on a ghost train, ate toffee apples and, all in all, he
....

4
Adrian and Melanie had already got three sons, so when Alexandra was born they were overjoyed, especially Adrian who had always wanted a daughter. As far as Adrian was concerned, Alexandra could do nothing wrong. In fact, she was ....

5
We gave a party last Saturday for some friends of ours. My uncle, who's seventy-five, happened to be staying with us so we naturally asked him to join the party. We didn't think he'd enjoy it very much but it was amazing. He laughed, told jokes, danced, ate and drank and was definitely
....

PROGRESS TEST UNITS 36–40

1 Complete each sentence so that it means the same as the preceding sentence.

1 She's always using my perfume without asking.

I wish ....

....

2 It wasn't very polite of him not to let us know in advance.

He might ....

....

3 I wish he wouldn't use the phone when I want to use it.

He's always ....

....

4 You mustn't lean out of the train window.

On no account ....

....

5 Bill is aggressive and sarcastic.

Not only ....

....

6 I had just got into the shower when the doorbell rang.

No sooner ....

....

7 It amazes me that people are so unconcerned about the famine in Africa.

What amazes ....

....

8 Don't worry about him. It's pointless.

There's no point ....

....

2 Complete the sentences with the correct form of the word in capital letters.

1 He drove fast cars and liked to live

.... DANGER

2 She gave a beautiful .... of the Mozart clarinet concerto. INTERPRET

3 .... , the best actor was not chosen for the part in the film. FORTUNE

4 Sylvia has become a very rich and successful

romantic .... NOVEL

5 I .... don't know what to do about it. HONEST

6 Young people are very .... aware nowadays. POLITICS

7 She was .... at the way she was treated at the bank. FURY

8 The plane crashed into the sea but

.... everyone survived. MIRACLE

3 Circle A, B, or C to indicate the word or phrase which best completes each sentence.

1 The twins were ... and no one could tell them apart.
A same B like C alike D identical

2 The climbers ... to reach the summit in three days.
A managed B arrived C succeeded D got

3 In my ..., the book is one of the best she's written so far.
A mind B meaning C intention D opinion

4 She stopped at a ... petrol station to ask the way.
A near B nearest C nearby D next

5 I really could do ... a nice cup of tea.
A without B away with C up D with

6 The child has a very ... imagination.
A lively B alive C living D live

7 You've arrived ... ! We've been waiting for ages.
A at last B in the end C at least D eventually

8 It's not ... spending so much money on a holiday.
A use B point C worth D sense

Areas of difficulty in speechwork

PRONUNCIATION TABLE

Consonants		Vowels	
symbol	*keyword*	*symbol*	*keyword*
/b/	**b**ark	/iː/	l**ea**ve
/d/	**d**o	/ɪ/	l**i**ve
/ð/	**th**is	/i/	eas**y**
/dʒ/	**j**ust	/e/	m**e**n
/f/	**f**it	/æ/	f**a**t
/g/	**g**ot	/ɑː/	h**ar**d
/h/	**h**at	/ɒ/	n**o**t
/j/	**y**et	/ɔː/	f**our**
/k/	**k**itchen	/ʊ/	c**ou**ld
/l/	**l**ook	/u/	sit**u**ation
/m/	**m**ay	/uː/	barbec**ue**
/n/	**n**ose	/ʌ/	r**u**b
/ŋ/	ri**ng**	/ɜː/	g**ir**l
/p/	**p**at	/ə/	fath**er**
/r/	**r**ed	/eɪ/	w**ai**st
/s/	**s**ee	/əʊ/	w**o**ke
/ʃ/	wi**sh**	/aɪ/	m**igh**t
/t/	**t**alk	/aʊ/	n**ow**
/tʃ/	**ch**ip	/ɔɪ/	t**oy**
/θ/	**th**ink	/ɪə/	h**ere**
/v/	**v**ery	/eə/	th**ere**
/w/	**w**ell	/ʊə/	t**our**
/x/	lo**ch**	/uə/	man**ua**l
/z/	**z**oo	/eɪə/	pl**ayer**
/ʒ/	plea**s**ure	/əʊə/	l**ower**
		/aɪə/	f**ire**
		/aʊə/	fl**ower**
		/ɔɪə/	empl**oyer**

A WEAK FORMS

1 Questions

Most auxiliary verbs have a weak pronunciation form as well as a strong pronunciation form. The weak form is generally used in questions.

e.g. Where **does** he work? /dəz/

Where **were** you born? /wə/

Note

Some British speakers use weak forms of auxiliaries when starting questions, but the strong form is also acceptable.

e.g. **Does** he work here? /dəz/ or /dʌz/

Can she type? /kən/ or /kæn/

Listen and repeat the questions.

When do they start? When shall I come?
What can she say? Who could he ask?
Why was he there? Why should I pay?

2 Modal verbs in the past

In the past form of modal verbs, *have* is usually pronounced as a weak form.

e.g. She might **have** lost it. /əv/

Listen and repeat the sentences.

They might have caught a different train.
He must have found it by now.
She can't have finished the book yet.
I could have sworn he was there.

3 Grammar words

Small 'grammar-like' words are generally pronounced in their weak form in connected speech, e.g. *a, an, the, some, and, but, to, of, at, from, that, than, as.*

e.g. A coat **of** paint /ə kəʊt əv peɪnt/

I want **to** go. /aɪ wɒntə gəʊ/

as soon **as** I can /əz suːn əz aɪ kæn/

some bread **and** butter /səm bred ən bʌtə/

Listen and repeat the sentences.

I have to leave.
It's not the time of day to do it.
I drove from home to work in twenty minutes.
I said that it was mine.
I bought some bread and milk at the shop.
It's cheaper than in London but not as cheap as I thought.

B CONTRACTIONS

Some auxiliaries have a contracted form, generally used in positive sentences.

e.g. **I'll** see you on Monday. /aɪl/

They've left already. /ðeɪv/

In negative sentences, the *not* is usually contracted to *n't* /ənt/ and added to the full form of the auxiliary.

e.g. I **wouldn't** like to live here. /wʊdənt/

I **haven't** got the time. /hævənt/

Listen and repeat the sentences.

I've already paid the bill.
She's coming on the ten o'clock train.
They weren't at home when I called.
You couldn't give me a hand, could you?
I think you've broken your arm.

C WORD LINKING

1 Sound liaison

When a word ending in a consonant sound is followed by a word beginning with a vowel sound, the two words are 'linked' together.
e.g. A **cup of** tea /kʌpəv/
The **girl is** French. /gɜːlɪz/
British speakers who do not pronounce the final *r* usually introduce it if the next word begins with a vowel.
e.g. mother **and** father /mʌðərənfɑːðə/

Listen and repeat the phrases and sentences.
a waste of time What a nice idea! How are you?
now and then high and low way out
here and there far and wide

2 Sound deletion

Some sounds are deleted or merged with other sounds in connected speech:

/t/ and /d/ are often deleted when they occur between two other consonants.
e.g. mus**t** be /mʌsbi/ stan**d** still /stænstɪl/

/t/ and /d/ are not pronounced clearly when followed by a /p/ or /b/.
e.g. bi**t** better /bɪpbetə/ goo**d** boy /gʊbbɔɪ/

/n/ is pronounced like /m/ before /p/ and /b/.
e.g. te**n** pence /tempens/ o**ne** boy /wʌmbɔɪ/

/n/ is pronounced like /ŋ/ before /k/.
e.g. o**n**e case /wʌŋkeɪs/ mai**n** clause /meɪŋklɔːz/

/s/ is pronounced like /ʃ/ before /j/ or /ʃ/.
e.g. thi**s** year /ðɪʃjɪə/ thi**s** shop /ðɪʃʃɒp/

/ə/ is sometimes lost in some multisyllable words.
e.g. different /dɪfrənt/ interesting /ɪntrəstɪŋ/

Listen and repeat the phrases.
must pay the fact that next day stand still
good point won't be ten points one bed
in case one card this shirt secretary
policeman library

D PRONOUNCIATION OF INDIVIDUAL SOUNDS

The following sounds, or pairs of sounds, often cause difficulty.

1 /ɪ/ hit /iː/ heat

Listen and practise the difference.
his/he's live/leave sit/seat hit/heat
fit/feet

Listen and underline the word you hear in each sentence.
1 leave/live 2 feel/fill 3 sheep/ship
4 beat/bit 5 we'll/will

Listen and repeat the sentences.
Please keep the streets clean.
What's this in Japanese?
Peter lives at sixty three Pitt Street.

2 /æ/ fat /ʌ/ sun

Listen and practise the difference.
hat/hut mad/mud run/ran drunk/drank
much/match

Listen and underline the word you hear in each sentence.
1 ankle/uncle 2 hut/hat 3 ran/run
4 crashed/crushed 5 rug/rag

Listen and repeat the phrases and sentences.
an African rug a mad uncle
a ham sandwich and a currant bun
She rang her mother on Monday, not Saturday.

3 /eɪ/ take /e/ said

Listen and practise the difference.
wait/wet main/men gate/get taste/test
late/let

Listen and underline the word you hear in each sentence.
1 debt/date 2 shed/shade 3 let/late
4 pepper/paper 5 pen/pain

Listen and repeat the sentences.
He's waiting to test it. It was a grey, wet day.
I'll fetch a pen straight away.

4 /əʊ/ road /ɔː/ door

Listen and practise the difference.
note/nought coat/caught low/law
bone/born cold/called

Listen and underline the word you hear in each sentence.
1 hole/hall 2 bowl/ball 3 loan/lawn
4 coal/call 5 snow/snore

Listen and repeat the phrases and sentences.
no more snow It won't be boring.
a phone call for Joe The water is cold.

5 /t/ ten /θ/ think /ð/ then /d/ den

Listen and practise the difference.
tin/thin part/path tank/thank tree/three
then/den there/dare breathe/breed
than/Dan

Listen and underline the word you hear in each sentence.
1 tin/thin 2 tree/three 3 Den/then
4 drew/threw 5 part/path 6 breed/breathe

Listen and repeat the phrases and sentences.
Danny's mother and father
This is the third time I've thanked her.
Take a deep breath and count to thirty.

6 /p/ **p**at /b/ **b**at /t/ **t**oo /d/ **d**o /k/ **c**url /g/ **g**irl

Listen and practise the difference.
pat/bat ton/done cot/got pet/bet
tore/door card/guard

Listen and underline the word you hear in each sentence.
1 pack/back 2 time/dime 3 peach/beach
4 tied/dyed 5 cold/gold 6 class/glass

Listen and repeat the phrases.
a cup of tea and a glass of milk
a piece of cake and a biscuit
a Burmese cat and a Pekinese dog
ninety pence for two peaches and a bunch of grapes

7 /b/ **b**erry /v/ **v**ery

Listen and practise the difference.
berry/very bain/vain ban/van best/vest
bet/vet bow/vow bat/vat beer/veer
boat/vote

Listen and repeat the phrases and sentences.
a rubber ball five friends of Bob
a very lively boy He visited Bilbao.
have a biscuit

8 /v/ **v**ary /w/ **w**ary

Listen and practise the difference.
veal/wheel vest/west via/wire vet/wet
vary/wary

Listen and underline the word you hear in each sentence.
1 vine/wine 2 vest/west 3 vet/wet
4 verse/worse

Listen and repeat the phrases and sentences.
a very wet winter a week's work
seven sandwiches We won't invite her.
William went to Vienna on Wednesday.

9 /r/ **r**ed /l/ **l**ight

Listen and practise the difference.
red/led right/light row/low read/lead
wrong/long

Listen and underline the word you hear in each sentence.
1 red/lead 2 long/wrong 3 light/right
4 glass/grass 5 glow/grow

Listen and repeat the phrases.
a red letter day green grass
the long road to London
the bright lights of Richmond

10 /s/ **s**end /z/ **z**oo

Listen and practise the difference.
ice/eyes lace/laze sue/zoo rice/rise
once/ones price/prize

Listen and underline the word you hear in each sentence.
1 said/zed 2 loose/lose 3 sip/zip
4 pence/pens 5 Sue's/zoos

Listen and repeat the sentences.
She's won first prize. It's freezing outside.
It's used for sailing. These are easy sentences.
I need a razor. He wants a rise in salary.

11 /s/ **s**aw /ʃ/ **s**ure /ʒ/ plea**s**ure

Listen and practise the sounds.
see she sell shell sock shock
press pressure pleasure cushion action
vision leisure measure usually beige

Listen and repeat the phrases and sentences.
six sheets She sells cushions.
I'm sure she sent it. She's at the leisure centre.
I usually read Shakespeare for pleasure.

12 the silent *r* /hɑːd/ **h**ard

Listen and repeat the words and sentences.
hard word girl port better father
sure wear cure fire iron earth
It's hard work. My father's sure to hear.
Where's the iron? The farmhouse is on fire.
You'd better wear my jacket.

13 Consonant clusters beginning with /s/ **st**udent

Listen and practise the sounds.
school stop student Spanish Scottish
slipped street stranger

Listen and repeat the sentences.
I started school at the age of six.
We spoke to some Spanish students.
She slipped in the street and strained her wrist.

14 /tr/ **tr**ain /dr/ **dr**ain /str/ **str**etch

Listen and practise the sounds.
try/dry train/drain trip/drip trill/drill
tread/dread trout/drought
stress strain stretch straw stripe
stroll strange

Listen and repeat the phrases and sentences.
a trip to Truro by train
He wore dreadful stripey trousers and a straw hat.
strangers strolling down the street
I tried to find something to drink.

Flairplan Phototypesetting Ltd
10299 Longman B/P Upper Inter. Matters W/B
Prelims
Vol 41 File 55 17/3/93 RJM

Longman Group UK Limited
Longman House, Burnt Mill, Harlow
Essex CM20 2JE, England
and Associated Companies throughout the world.

First published in 1993

Set in 9½/11pt Linotype Versailles

Printed in Spain by Mateu Cromo, S.A. Pinto (Madrid)

ISBN: 0 582 09910 2

Illustrated by Julie Douglas, Pauline Hazelwood, Ann Johns, David Parkins, Chris Pavely, Martin Salisbury

Acknowledgements
We are grateful to the following for permission to reproduce copyright material:
the author, Ruth Fainlight for her poem 'Handbag' from *Selected Poems* (pub Hutchinson, 1987); Random House UK Ltd for an adapted extract from *NSPCC Book of Famous Faux Pas* edited by Fiona Snelson (pub Hutchinson); Reader's Digest Association Ltd for an extract from the article 'Life's Like That' from *Reader's Digest* magazine, January 1987, © 1987 The Reader's Digest Association.

We are grateful to the following for permission to reproduce photographs:
Ace Photo Agency for page 18 (middle left); Art Directors Photolibrary for pages 49 (top) and 57; John Birdsall Photography for pages 5 and 53: Britstock-IFA Photolibrary for page 49 (below); J Allan Cash Ltd for pages 10, 12 (above and below), 18 (right) and 49 (middle); Greg Evans Photolibrary for page 18 (left); Mary Evans Picture Library for page 61; The Hutchison Library/Michael MacIntyre for pages 1 and 18 (middle right); The Image Bank for page 49 (above); Longman Photo Unit for page 40; Network Photographers/Mike Goldwater for page 23 and /John Sturrock for page 26; Plymouth News Pictures/Nic Randall for page 35; Rex Features Ltd for page 20; Tony Stone Worldwide for pages 56 and 62; Telegraph Colour Library for pages 8 and 32.